INTERSECTIONS

INTERSECTIONS

Post-Critical Studies in Preaching

Edited by

Richard L. Eslinger

WILLIAM B. EERDMANS PUBLISHING COMPANY
GRAND RAPIDS, MICHIGAN

© 1994 Wm. B. Eerdmans Publishing Co.
255 Jefferson Ave. S.E., Grand Rapids, Michigan 49503

Printed in the United States of America

00 99 98 97 96 95 94   7 6 5 4 3 2 1

Library of Congress Cataloging-in-Publication Data

Intersections: post-critical studies in preaching /
edited by Richard L. Eslinger.
p.   cm.
Includes bibliographical references.
ISBN 0-8028-0714-3 (pbk.)
1. Bible — Homiletical use.
I. Eslinger, Richard L. (Richard Laurence), 1940-
BS534.5.I54   1994
251 — dc20   94-19492
CIP

The editor and publisher wish to thank *Interpretation* magazine for permission to
reprint Joanna Dewey's article "Oral Methods of Structuring Narrative in Mark," which
first appeared in the January 1989 (vol. 43, no. 1) issue of that periodical.

Contents

CONTENTS

Dedicated to the lay theologians
of "Soup and Study" at
University Temple United Methodist Church,
1987-1992

Acknowledgments

I am deeply indebted to the members of University Temple United Methodist Church for their support in undertaking this project. Also, I am grateful to the people of Vancouver School of Theology in Vancouver, British Columbia, for the hospitality they extended to me when I was there doing research on the intersections of narrative and imagery. To my wife, Elise, and daughter, Catherine, I want to say "thank you" again for granting me space and time to do the work of an editor and author. Finally, for her conscientious work in typing this manuscript, I am indebted to Barbara Momeyer, and, for his equally able work as editor, I am also indebted to Tim Straayer.

Contributors

David Buttrick: Professor of Preaching, Vanderbilt Divinity School, Nashville, Tennessee.

Joanna Dewey: Professor of New Testament Studies, Episcopal Divinity School, Cambridge, Massachusetts.

Richard L. Eslinger: Visiting Scholar at Saint Meinrad School of Theology, St. Meinrad, Indiana, and pastor of Hatfield and Yankeetown United Methodist Churches.

David M. Greenhaw: Dean of Lancaster Theological Seminary, Lancaster, Pennsylvania.

Thomas G. Long: Professor of Preaching and Worship, Princeton Theological Seminary, Princeton, New Jersey.

Bernard Brandon Scott: Professor of New Testament, Phillips Graduate Theological Seminary, Tulsa, Oklahoma.

Thomas H. Troeger: Professor of Preaching and Communications, Iliff School of Theology, Denver, Colorado.

Editor's Introduction

Stanley Hauerwas described his work *Against the Nations* as one response to George Lindbeck's lament that "there is much talk at present about typological, figurative, and narrative theology, but little performance."[1] In a postliberal world, Hauerwas prophesies, the foundational assumptions, methodology, and subject matter of Christian ethics will look quite different. The move to a narrative-based Christian ethics is evidence of a paradigm shift.

This volume also speaks to new realities in a post-liberal, post-critical world — specifically, to the altered nature of interpretation and preaching. Both the theology and praxis of preaching have changed as a result of the fact that they are both ideologically rooted in the historical criticism of late nineteenth-century liberalism, especially in its accommodation to the new science and new historiography. Recent homiletical theory and praxis implicitly affirm that both historical-critical biblical interpretation and liberalism as a religious and cultural movement are well past the era of their ascendancy. We are very evidently post-liberal and post-critical, even if liberalism and historical criticism continue to exert a waning force in church and in culture. Something new is afoot, especially in the area of hermeneutics.

When historical criticism held sway as *the* interpretive paradigm within much of liberal Protestant and Roman Catholic biblical scholarship,

---

1. Lindbeck, *The Nature of Doctrine in a Postliberal Age* (Philadelphia: Westminster Press, 1984), p. 135. Hauerwas quotes Lindbeck in *Against the Nations: War and Society in a Liberal Society* (New York: Winston Press, 1985), p. 1.

it maintained an easy marriage with a general model of homiletics. Historical criticism would deliver a "world" behind the text, and preaching could then attend to the "message" or meaning within that world. Generations of preachers were trained to make the passage from a text's main idea to a full sermonic outline of that idea's subpoints and illustrations. One "built" or "crafted" the sermon on the essential theme discovered behind the biblical text.

All of the contributors to this volume agree that this marriage is over and that the old discursive homiletics is no longer tenable. Some believe historical-critical methodology still has some value, but only as it is bracketed by and supplemented with other interpretive approaches. Others of us, as David Buttrick notes, concur with Walter Wink's assertion that "historical biblical criticism is bankrupt." Whether adopting "soft" or "hard" post-critical positions, each contributor has seen an emerging new criticism — literary, phenomenological, structuralist, or the like — as offering a way beyond the collapsed historical-critical project. For them the challenge is to chart new directions for homiletics within the contexts of these new interpretive models.

The contributors to this volume have adopted the methodology of developing their interpretive foundations at some length and then exploring the implications of these foundations for the ministry of preaching. As each writer leads us through these hermeneutic and homiletic explorations, he or she initiates a dialogue with the other contributors. Tom Long questions the adequacy of literary criticism and the historical model to deal adequately with apocalyptic. Yet all of the contributors are indebted to the insights of literary criticism. Joanna Dewey concurs with Walter Ong about the impact of orality on narrative plot, asserting that linear plot development is not a dominant characteristic of oral narratives. Yet David Buttrick grounds his homiletic in the confidence that biblical texts yield up plots that want to function with some sequential logic in consciousness. On the other hand, Buttrick has elsewhere challenged the narrative hermeneuts (Scott and myself, at least), arguing that narrative is inadequate by itself as an interpretive stance. There is a "symbolic-reflective" dimension to Christian faith that intersects with the narrative story line of Scripture, he says — the living symbol of Jesus Christ.[2]

In response to Buttrick's argument, David Greenhaw pleads for a chastened retention of the notion of concept within a post-critical homiletic.

2. Buttrick, *Homiletic* (Philadelphia: Fortress Press, 1987), pp. 13-17.

Drawing on the work of Craddock and utilizing Ricoeur's insights into the act of interpretation, Greenhaw argues for a reclamation of the *concept* as the basis for what is preached. Tom Troeger, however, insists that any homiletical reconstruction must take into account post-modern poetics. Rather than viewing "the turbulent state of biblical interpretation, theology and hermeneutics" as "yet another attack on God and the integrity of God's Word," Troeger contends that "the post-modern shift in the poetics of theological expression represents nothing less than a revelation from God."

The contributions by Bernard Brandon Scott and myself both acknowledge the efficacy of narrative hermeneutics but expand the trajectory of interpretation in different directions. Scott looks to the interplay between biblical and contemporary stories as an essential context for preaching. He outlines the redemptive myth of the solo savior in the Dirty Harry film series and shows how New Testament christology challenges that myth. I argue that a narrative hermeneutic has to be complemented by a rhetoric of imagery. Text and image both provide essential coordinates for the interpretation of God's self-disclosure in Jesus Christ.

Each contributor to this collection also stands in dialogue with other scholars seeking to develop a post-critical hermeneutics. Long indirectly speaks with Elisabeth Schüssler-Fiorenza concerning her presentation of apocalyptic as an alternative symbolic universe.[3] Dewey continues a conversation with such Markan literary critics as Keller, Rhoads, and Malbon, building on their work but insisting that attention to Mark's essentially oral rhetoric qualifies judgments as to the valuation of the disciples, the short ending, and the disconnectedness of Mark's plot. William Lynch reminds Greenhaw and me that "the world of the imagination is compact with *ideas,* so compact indeed that they cannot be sorted out from the images."[4] As Fr. Lynch bluntly puts it, "Images think."

Finally, each of us is in dialogue with you the reader, and especially you the preacher. It is to equip you in your vocation that we do our own work. Faith still comes through hearing.

RICHARD L. ESLINGER

---

3. See Schüssler-Fiorenza, *The Book of Revelation: Justice and Judgment* (Philadelphia: Fortress Press, 1985).

4. Lynch, "Religion and the Literary Imagination," *Religion and Literature: The Convergence of Approaches,* JAAR Thematic Studies, vol. 47, June 1979, p. 335.

The Preacher and the Beast:
From Apocalyptic Text to Sermon

Thomas G. Long

"Apocalyptic," Ernst Käsemann once announced, "is the mother of all Christian theology." If there is any truth at all in that statement, then it is also true that most Christian preaching has become at least slightly embarrassed by its mother, especially over the strange things she has written. Aside from the eyeball-rolling, delusional fringe characters who comb through Daniel, Revelation, and other apocalyptic materials searching for covert references to Roosevelt, Hitler, the Ayatollah, the Common Market, and the coming Armageddon in the Near East, most preachers would probably be happy never to have to wrangle with any biblical text that features a beast with ten horns and claws of bronze, stars falling from the heavens, a great red dragon with seven heads, or the enigmatic number 666. Apocalyptic may be our mother, but at this late date mother seems to be growing a bit daft.

Much of the great tradition of critical biblical scholarship shares this preacher's distaste for things apocalyptic. A product of "late Judaism," sniffed Wellhausen and Schürer; "a suspicious symptom of tendencies toward heresy," moaned Ebeling, jabbing at Käsemann.[1] Lectionary editors, for their part, cheerfully comply with the preacher's desire to avoid the more bizarre examples of apocalyptic texts. The Common Lectionary, for example, includes a few slices of apocalyptic material from the synop-

---

1. Cf. John J. Collins, *The Apocalyptic Imagination: An Introduction to the Jewish Matrix of Christianity* (New York: Crossroad Books, 1984), p. 1.

1

tics, but only three lessons from Daniel are listed, and the few lessons included from Revelation are all drawn from the relatively gentler hymnic sections of that book. One can travel blithely through the lectionary never opening any bottomless pit, never encountering sulphur belching from a mount, never seeing the moon drip blood, and never running into a beast making war on the saints.

So the prevailing tendencies of classical biblical scholarship, the pruning shears of lectionary editors, and the understandable reluctance of most preachers to go one-on-one with cryptic texts have conspired to reduce the apocalyptic voice to a whisper in most pulpits. On the one hand, this is hardly a cause for alarm. Biblical knowledge among the general populace has evaporated to the point that many people would not be able to distinguish between Jeremiah and a geranium, much less be concerned about troop movements at Armageddon. Preachers nowadays do well to introduce their hearers to the very simplest of biblical images and themes and can hardly be faulted for not asking their congregations to mount the wild horses of the apocalypse.

On the other hand, this loss of the apocalyptic voice in preaching is much to be lamented. To be sure, apocalyptic is not the *only* voice in the Christian chorus, but it is, I hope to show, an important voice. It is sometimes a dissonant and unwelcome voice, and the lyrics it chooses are often indecipherable, but on certain occasions and in certain circumstances, if the Christian faith cannot make apocalyptic sounds, it has little to sing.

My aim, then, is to explore what this "apocalyptic voice" might be in contemporary preaching — that is, to assess the possibility of recovering responsible preaching based on apocalyptic biblical texts. In order to do this, we will naturally need to look carefully at the nature and purpose of biblical apocalyptic literature. But our task is much larger than that. Before we can know how to preach the apocalyptic genre of texts in particular, we must reexamine what it means more generally to preach from *any* biblical text.

Indeed, the thorny problems faced by a preacher encountering an apocalyptic biblical text can serve as a test case for the prevailing methods of biblical preaching. Much of the perplexity preachers feel when faced with an apocalyptic text is generated by the fact that many conventional text-to-sermon methods are factory defective. The fact that these methods appear to function fairly well for most "ordinary" texts simply hides their inherent flaws and obscures what is actually taking place when a preacher manages to employ them to move from text to sermon. When an "extraordinary" text, such as an apocalyptic pericope, is placed in the customary exegetical winepress, out pours harsh vinegar, and so the text, naturally, is discarded. The problem is usually not with the texts but with the text-to-sermon machinery. Our particular quest to recover the apocalyptic voice in preaching, then, is bracketed by a larger concern to articulate a more adequate way to move from text to sermon in general.

Garden Variety Exegesis

Consider the situation of a typical preacher beginning to work on the interpretation of a biblical text in preparation for a sermon. The preacher knows that the text is not going to whisper "Now this is what I want you to tell them on Sunday." The text must be *interpreted,* which means, of course, that the preacher must *do* something to the text — study it, analyze it, "listen" to it, something. Now, most preachers have learned in seminary or elsewhere some version of what to do; the standard procedures of exegesis are well known. Moreover, most preachers will also be aware of the dangers of *eisegesis,* the tendency to "read into" a text what we want it to say rather than drawing out of the text what it wishes to say. Preachers, then, approach their texts like surgeons, with analytical scalpels and interpretive forceps in hand, instruments that they hope are as sterile and nonintrusive as possible.

Even so, before any work is done on the text per se, before any word of the text is examined, before the first commentary is consulted, in fact even before the text in question is read, the preacher already has made some prior judgments about the text. No interpretive process is sterile or value-free. In the first place, the very fact that he or she is planning to base a sermon on the results of the exegesis indicates that the preacher assumes that something about this text will prove to have contemporary relevance. Most of us make that assumption about a text's potential pertinence fairly casually, actually as a matter of course, when in truth it embodies a rather dramatic claim about the text as Scripture.[2] By contrast,

2. David Nineham, for one, does not think that it is self-evident that a biblical text will prove to have a contemporary meaning. Speaking of this assumption on the part of preachers and biblical students, he says, "Many statements in ancient texts have *no*

hardly anyone would assume that some random snippet of ancient writing
— a couple of lines from a Jebusite battle account, say — would have any
important word to speak to modern people. But we routinely (and correctly, in my view) expect this of biblical texts.

The preacher also brings an assumption — perhaps even a presumption — about the nature of the biblical text as text. Most preachers
would readily admit at the beginning of an exegesis that they don't know
what the text in question *means,* and yet they do believe that they know
what kind of thing the text *is.* The problem is that most of us have been
trained to think too narrowly about the nature of a biblical text, and this
works various kinds of mischief in interpretation. Our assumptions cause
us to look at the text only in certain ways and thus to miss what the text
may be generating outside our range of vision. To borrow a leaf from
Kierkegaard, if we see a sign in a shop window that reads "We Sell and
Repair Watches," most of us would infer that this is a jeweler's shop. Maybe
so, but if we applied another frame of reference, we could infer that this
is a shop that makes signs. The assumptions we make before we look at
a text exercise a surprising and risky degree of control over the meaning
we can eventually find in that text.

What do preachers assume about the nature of texts? When it comes
to the actual operations of exegesis, we tend to apply one of two broad
frames of reference to the text.

1. The most widespread and "commonsense" view of biblical texts
(actually rather a modern view in the sweep of biblical interpretation) is
that texts are historical documents. This does not imply that texts are not
theologically loaded, that they cannot speak "spiritual truths," or that
everything in them is historically "true" in the contemporary sense. What
it does mean is that biblical texts are assumed to be the records of things
said or written by historical persons to other persons in particular historical
settings. Thus, the main interpretive questions appropriate to ask a biblical
text are, quite naturally, historical ones: Who said this, when, to whom,
and in what setting?

Take, as an example, the text popularly know as the parable of the

---

meaning today in the normal sense of the word 'meaning.' No doubt if you reflect long
enough over any ancient statement — even, let us say, an historical inaccuracy in some
ancient Egyptian annals — interesting reflections of some sort will occur to you; but my
colleagues seemed to mean something more positive and direct than that" ("The Bible in
Modern Theology," *Bulletin of the John Rylands Library* 52 [1954]: 181).

Prodigal Son (Luke 15:11-32). Who said this text to whom, and in what circumstances? One possible answer is that this text, just as Luke presents it, is a story uttered by Jesus to the Pharisees and scribes in the midst of a conflict over Jesus' style of ministry. Or one may speculate that Luke has taken this story out of its original context and that the story was originally told by Jesus in some other ministry setting. At the very least, one would view this text as a narrative about Jesus telling a parable, a story that Luke told to his readers. Perhaps one would consider the text to be some combination of these possibilities, but, in every case, the text is seen historically. The assumption is made that the parable was communicated by some historical figure (Jesus, Luke, or both) in some historical setting (Jesus', Luke's, or both), and the primary meaning of the text is to be found in that setting.

Any preacher who makes such an assumption about texts faces the question of how to transfer textual meaning from one historical setting (the text's) to another (that of the preacher and the contemporary congregation). What does it *mean* to us that the text once *meant* thus and so to other people? Preachers and their biblical scholar allies have devised all sorts of means for making this transfer. The two most often employed are: (a) finding some central idea in the text that can travel through time ("God is a loving and forgiving parent") or (b) forging some sort of dynamic analogy between the historical circumstances of the text and our own circumstances ("We see ourselves, don't we, in the hardened faces of those scribes and Pharisees. Aren't we so often just like them?").

2. Under the influence of the more recent forms of literary criticism in biblical studies, some preachers have lately begun to replace the historical view of texts with an aesthetic one. In the same way that one can be moved by the dramatic power of a Shakespearean play even if one knows nothing about its historical origins, they say, so the poetic force of biblical texts transcends the historical circumstances of their creation. On this basis they contend that the meanings of biblical texts should be sought not in their histories but rather in the texts themselves, in the "language worlds" they create.

As for the parable of the Prodigal Son, they would say, it matters little whether Jesus uttered this story to the Pharisees, to the disciples, to the birds of the air, or not at all. Whether Luke's first readers were rich or poor, obedient or prodigal, doubting or faithful is of small consequence. The task of the preacher is not to roam around backstage trying to ascertain the history behind the text but to invite the hearers of the sermon onto the stage of the parable itself, to guide them down the passageways of its plot, to experience the architecture of its characters and symbols, to feel the contrast between the artistic and theological world contained in the text and the "routine" world outside.

There is much truth and genuine value in these two views of biblical texts, and it must be admitted that they have served the enterprise of biblical preaching fairly well. Toss them a fastball, like a good old David narrative, a parable, or a healing story, and they can knock it over the fence. Mix in a screwball, however, like an apocalyptic text, and they flail at the air. Hurl a passage like Daniel 7 at the historically oriented preachers, and they quickly fall into the role of explainers: "Now, look, this fourth beast, the one that has ten horns and then a little horn growing up and plucking out three of the other horns — we're not really sure exactly what this means. The ten horns refer to rulers, but which ones, I can't say. Some Seleucids maybe, a few Ptolemies perhaps, but we are fairly confident that the little horn is Antiochus IV Epiphanes. You history students will remember that Antiochus. . . ." Any possible connection between the text and the contemporary world is lost among the minute historical references necessary to the intricate process of deciphering the code. Invite aesthetically oriented preachers text, and they will suddenly find themselves in a surrealistic little shop of horrors. The winds are blowing, the sea is churning, and crawling across the landscape are a lion with eagle's wings, a bear chewing three ribs in its teeth, and a four-headed monster. Forget art; most preachers would be glad to escape that realm with their sanity, much less a sermon.

Change Frames

If we are to salvage apocalyptic and other unwieldy texts for preaching, we will need a new frame of reference, some alternative way of understanding the nature of a text and its potential relationship to a sermon. Neither the historical nor the aesthetic understanding of a text, standing alone, is adequate to account for its depths or formative powers. I want to suggest that a biblical text can best be viewed as *performative language.*[3]

3. Paul Ricoeur also employs the concept of biblical language as "performative," and he specifically applies this to apocalyptic texts in his foreword to André Lacocque's *The Book of Daniel,* trans. David Pellauer (Atlanta: John Knox Press, 1979), pp. xvii-xxvi.

What this means is that biblical texts are attempts (to borrow a phrase from John Searle) "to do things with words." In a biblical text something is said in order to accomplish some purpose; texts are inserted into social systems with the intention of levying a force on those systems to create change. Meaning in texts occurs at the intersection between what is said and the forceful intention embodied in the language of the text.

For example, let us suppose that you and I are talking, and you say to me, "The door is wide open." Now, what does that mean? In part, it means just what you said: some door is wide open. There is more to the meaning than this, however, and the rest of the meaning depends on the context of our conversation. If we are, at the time, strolling through the neighborhood and you are pointing at the house of a neighbor who is away on vacation, you are trying to convey puzzlement, suspicion, even alarm at the fact that the neighbor's door is wide open. Moreover, you are trying to arouse that same reaction in me. But if we are sitting in your office and I have just launched into a juicy and confidential tale, your telling me that the door is wide open is your way of urging me either to lower my voice or to get up and close the door in order to ensure privacy. In short, when you say "The door is wide open," you are not merely transmitting a piece of information about a door; you are trying to *do* something with that information.

So, if I am truly to understand what you are saying to me, I must not only comprehend your words; I must also discern the implied effect of what you are saying. Putting this in a fancier way, to interpret your words, I must discern what force they exert on the communicational and social system into which they are uttered. At first glance, this may seem to say that I must be able both to hear your words and to read your mind in order to know what you're saying. Actually this is somewhat misleading. People have intentions, of course, and their words are expressions of those intentions, but, as our Sunday School teachers warned us, once we say things, we cannot get them back. We can supply more words as clarification, but once words are spoken into the context of a certain situation, they carry their own performative power. This is especially true in written communication, since the creator of a written text will not typically be present to provide clarification when it is read.

The degree to which spoken or written words are autonomous (i.e., free from the intentionality of the people who speak or write them) is, of course, a complex matter, but, without pressing the point too finely, we can say that the balance of meaning falls cleanly on the side of the words themselves rather than on the intentions of the speaker or writer. Meaning is to be found in the utterance or the text itself, not in our speculations about what may have been going on inside the head of the writer or speaker. If someone yells "Fire!" in a crowded theater, the most important thing from the crowd's perspective will be the intrinsic power of the word to create pandemonium in that context, not whatever might be going on inside the shouter's head.

In the same way, biblical texts both *say* things and *do* things. We do not have to read the mind of Paul or Luke (as if we could) in order to discern what a text written by one of them is saying and doing, but we do have to pay close attention to the language patterns of the text in relation to its context. In short, what a text *means* is a product of what it says and does in a given setting.

So, how do we find that out? One way to do this is to explore how the text may have fit into what we can reconstruct of its original historical setting, and here the historically oriented preachers were on the right track. When the writer of the Epistle of James says, "Come now, you rich, weep and howl for the miseries that are coming upon you" (5:1), it makes a considerable difference in communicational effect whether the first readers of James were themselves rich or poor. If they were rich, it could be argued that the performative effect of the text is to create fear; if they were poor (which is more likely the case), it could be argued that the function of the text is to generate hope and a gleeful anticipation of seeing their wealthy adversaries get it in the end. Likewise, if we think of the parable of the Prodigal Son as a speech-act directed toward an audience of scribes and Pharisees, it carries one effect; if we think of Luke's first readers as the audience, listening in as Jesus tells the parable to the scribes and Pharisees, it has another effect. Making some broad judgment about the probable historical contexts of a text, then, is a key step in determining textual meaning. Sometimes it is impossible to determine much at all about a text's *Sitz im Leben,* but usually there are enough internal and external clues to make a responsible judgment.

Another critical context that must be considered is that of the structure of the larger document in which a text appears. This can be done in terms of deep structure (employing structuralist methods), but I have more in mind here the surface sequences and patterns in which the overall document is arranged. As an example of the latter, suppose that we are reading a novel and we encounter a scene in which a man presents a diamond necklace to his wife as an anniversary gift and then embraces her, apparently with loving tenderness. Taken by itself, that scene could well touch and move us with its romantic charm. But if we had learned in a previous passage that the same man had secretly hired someone to murder her, we will not be touched by his embrace but enraged at his evil schemes and cruel hypocrisy. In other words, the effect of the later passage depends on what we have already learned in the novel.

In like manner, biblical texts take their places in the constellation of the larger documents to which they belong. For example, reading the story in John 11 about the raising of Lazarus, we come across the words "[Jesus] cried with a loud voice, 'Lazarus, come out.' The dead man came out" (vv. 43-44). The fact that earlier in the Gospel, in the midst of a discussion about the final resurrection and judgment, we hear Jesus saying, "Do not marvel at this; for the hour is coming when all who are in the tombs will hear his voice and come forth" (5:28-29a) causes the later text, through its resonance with the earlier one, to have an even more specific theological meaning than it has standing alone.

A final context to be considered is that of the act of reading, especially as governed by literary genre. When people write things, they do not merely string along words and ideas in sequence; they fit the words and ideas into certain conventional patterns called *genres*.[4] I begin most of my letters "Dear ————," even if the recipient ("Dear IRS") is not particularly dear to me. I do this because that is the accepted generic custom for letters in our culture. People in our culture who read written communications that begin "Dear ————" know instantly that the documents are letters, as opposed to news reports or theological essays, and they set their reading expectations accordingly.

It is important to know the genre of a biblical text because genre provides clues to the potential effect of the text. Since a genre constitutes an implied invitation to the reader to read the text this way rather than that, genres tend to create predictable effects upon readers. We can see this most clearly in simple genres. For instance, the highly regularized pattern of a joke (setup — complication — surprise punch line) is a genre

---

4. John Barton provides this more precise definition of *genre*: "A *Gattung* or genre is a conventional pattern, recognizable by certain formal criteria (style, shape, tone, or even grammatical structures, recurring formulaic patterns), which is used in a particular society in social contexts which are governed by certain formal conventions" (*Reading the Old Testament: Method in Biblical Study* [Philadelphia: Westminster Press, 1984], p. 32).

aimed at producing laughter. A riddle is designed to puzzle, a ghost story to frighten, and so on.[5]

A reader's interaction with any genre is largely a matter of poetics — by which I mean the capacity of the language and internal machinery of the text to create certain effects in a cooperative reader. In this regard, the aesthetic critics were on the right track, although, contrary to their assertions, a literary genre cannot entirely be divorced from its sociocultural setting. Genres transcend particular settings (jokes are built the same way in Paris and Peoria), but they do have cultural and historical life spans (virtually every modern American reader would recognize the "limerick" genre, but not so an ancient Assyrian). If I am going to understand the effects of a biblical genre, I must know something about how the original recipients of the text would have engaged its genre.

So what are preachers supposed to look for as they interpret biblical texts? They are not merely to look for theological ideas floating in a historical soup, nor are they to look for timeless and universal aesthetic literary experiences. They are rather to look for the *action* of the text, what the text was *doing* in a specific historical setting.

Apocalyptic Revisited

Now that we have sketched the broad outlines of a performative approach to the interpretation of biblical texts, let us return to the original problem: preaching from apocalyptic texts. We will take, as a sample text, Revelation 12, a passage that possesses all the characteristic features of apocalyptic that prove so forbidding to the standard preacher's exegesis: enigmatic symbols (a woman clothed in the sun and stars with the moon at her feet), a well-stocked menagerie[6] (a great red dragon with seven heads and ten horns, a lamb, and a great eagle), and fantastic events (a war in heaven, the earth opening its mouth to consume a river of water pouring out of the mouth of the dragon). What we are going to try to do with this strange

---

5. For a more detailed examination of the relationship of literary genre to biblical preaching, see Thomas G. Long, *Preaching and the Literary Forms of the Bible* (Philadelphia: Fortress Press, 1988).

6. Luke Johnson, *The Writings of the New Testament* (Philadelphia: Fortress Press, 1986), p. 515.

text is to determine its performative function — that is, what the text *does* by virtue of what it *says*.

1. In terms of the *literary context* of our passage, Revelation 12 falls in the middle of the third and longest of the four major sections of the book of Revelation. In the first section (chap. 1), the writer announces that what follows is "the revelation [apocalypse] of Jesus Christ" that was given to the writer by God through an angel. Among other things, this already signals to the readers that they are reading an "apocalypse." Indeed, one of the identifying marks of the apocalyptic genre is that it involves "a narrative framework, in which a revelation is mediated by an otherworldly being to a human recipient."[7] I will have more to say about the features of this genre later.

The second section (chaps. 2–3) contains poetic but nonetheless fairly clear and direct letters to "the seven churches." Each letter is unique and makes specific reference to aspects of the life of the community addressed, but all seven letters share an identical structure.[8]

The third section (4:1–22:5), which includes our sample text, is inaugurated by the writer's report of passing through an open door in heaven (4:1). "Once the seer passes through the open door of heaven," observes Luke Johnson, "he and the readers are swept into a phantasmagorical world quite unlike any other. The visions of Revelation are dazzling in their imagery, if not altogether coherent."[9] In this section the throne of heaven is displayed, white-robed multitudes sing hymns of praise to the Lamb, plagues rage across the face of the earth, beasts of various sorts wreak havoc, Babylon falls, and a new heaven and a new earth are seen. These imagistic fireworks are followed by the fourth and final section (22:6-21), essentially containing exhortations and warnings about what should be done with the words of this book and the promise of Christ's imminent return.

Taken as a whole, then, the structure of the book of Revelation takes the reader on a dramatic roller coaster ride. It begins in the clouds at the top of a hill and then swoops down in the letters to the earthbound situations of the seven churches, only to swing back up into the supernatural ether of otherworldly symbols and then down once more to the tangible world of church life. The effect is jarring, unsettling, perhaps even

---

7. Collins, *The Apocalyptic Imagination,* p. 4.
8. Johnson, *The Writings of the New Testament,* pp. 524-25.
9. Johnson, *The Writings of the New Testament,* p. 525.

curiously riveting. It is something like listening to a bearded eccentric on a park bench muttering vague and indecipherable prophecies about the end of the world only to have him suddenly look up and ask you if you happen to know how the Mets did last night. The incongruity between the fantastic and the mundane forces you to decide whether you are dealing with a true crank or whether his seemingly disconnected prophecies might just be more fully grounded in a grasp of everyday reality than you are initially inclined to suppose.

2. Now we come to the question of genre, of what *reading process* the first readers of this text would have employed. They were members of what scholars call the "Johannine community," and one thing this means is that they were Christians who included among their treasured writings the Gospel of John and the Epistles of John. They were accustomed to the symbols and syntax of John's Gospel and the Epistles, although clearly they could not have read Revelation using the same reading style they employed for those documents.

Genre imposes certain demands on reading. I cannot make any sense of a Dylan Thomas poem if I try to read it using the same expectations and interpretive procedures that I use to read the sports page in the morning newspaper. No one even has to identify the genre of the poem for me to know that I have to read it differently. I instinctively know that it's a poem, and I switch reading techniques accordingly. Even if I had never encountered a poem before, never heard of poetry, the language, shape, and style of the text would signal to me that something new was demanded of me as a reader.

Just so, the genre of Revelation demanded of the Johannine community a reading style different from that demanded by the Gospel of John. They may well have known other apocalyptic writings and thus recognized the literary genre of Revelation, but even if they did not, the language and semantic structure of the text would have signaled the need for a different process of reading. In the first place, through its visionary and fantastic language, Revelation lifts readers out of their present situation and ushers them into an imaginative future world. The vocabulary stretches the boundaries of ordinary language, and almost every event and description practically screams at the reader, "This is *not* the present, everyday world you know and experience." As John Barton has observed, the reader of an apocalyptic text instinctively knows that a sentence that begins "The stars will fall from heaven, the sun will cease it shining, and the moon will drip blood" is not likely to end "the rest of the country will be partly cloudy with scattered showers."[10] Apocalyptic takes us into a world not our own.

But the reader's experience of being transported to another world is not all there is to the dynamics of reading Revelation. Here and there, dotted through the text, there are unmistakable, if not always completely clear, references to the present world of the reader. Now what happens to a reader who is bumping along, following the lead of the text, believing that he or she is taking a fantastic voyage through the future only to crash into unexpected reminders of the world at hand? Two possibilities: one, the reader may say "Ah, I get it. This isn't *really* about the future at all. It's really about the present, but it's written in hidden, coded, future-sounding languages." That would suggest that the reader's task is to crack the code, to reduce all of the illusory future references to their proper present tense. But, what if (and this is the case with Revelation) most of the language will not reduce and refuses to be cracked? What if many of the symbols and images resist all attempts to bring them to the earthbound realities of the present? That introduces the second reading possibility — namely, that the present and future tenses stand in tension side-by-side in the text, becoming mutually interpreting realities. The otherworldly and future dimensions of the text are applied metaphorically to the this-worldly and the present, and vice versa.[11]

To cite an explicit example, the reader of Revelation (chap. 4) is transported through time into the very presence of the enthroned and victorious God, whose presence is "like jasper and carnelian" and who is encircled by twenty-four white-clad elders with golden crowns upon their heads. From this throne come "flashes of lightning, and voices and peals of thunder." There is simply no possible way to domesticate such a scene, no means to get one's bearings in this landscape, and yet . . . and yet the hymns being sung in this throne room of a time-yet-to-be are the very same hymns sung so often in the Lord's Day liturgy of the Johannine church, "Holy, holy, holy is the Lord God Almighty" and "Worthy is the Lamb who was slain," and the image of the Lamb itself throws the reader back onto the familiar rhythms of the Gospel of John: "Behold the Lamb

10. Barton, *Reading the Old Testament,* p. 17.

11. Discussing the role of eschatology in biblical literature, G. B. Caird notes that "biblical writers believed literally that the world had had a beginning in the past and would have an end in the future" but that they also "regularly used end-of-the-world language metaphorically to refer to that which they knew was not the end of the world" (*The Language and Imagery of the Bible* [London: Duckworth, 1980], p. 256).

of God." The this-worldly worship of the heavenly court joins present and future into a simultaneous event of praise.

In our sample text, Revelation 12, the same dynamics are at work. The scene is set in heaven. A woman appears clothed in the garb of apocalyptic symbolism: the sun, moon, and stars. The woman is in the final pangs of childbirth, but just as she is about to deliver the child, a seven-headed, ten-horned dragon appears on the landscape, poised to devour the child when it is born. The woman bears the child, a son, who is described as one "who is to rule all the nations," and the newborn child is quickly "caught up to God and to his throne." The woman flees into the wilderness, to "a place prepared by God," where she is nourished for "one thousand two hundred and sixty days." Michael and his angelic troops show up to make war on the dragon and his legions, and the dragon is defeated and thrown down to the earth. The warfare in heaven is thus ended, and a victory cry goes out: "Now the salvation and the power and the kingdom of our God and the authority of his Christ have come, for the accuser of our brethren has been thrown down, who accuses them day and night before our God. And they have conquered him by the blood of the Lamb."

All is well in heaven, then, but not so on earth. The defeated dragon still has a few poisonous lashes left in his tail. He pursues the woman who bore the child, but she is given the means to escape. Angered, the dragon turns his fury on the "other offspring" of the woman, "those who keep the commandments of God and bear testimony to Jesus." At this point, the text abruptly ends, and the description of another vision begins.

The first readers of this text did not need sophisticated literary techniques to negotiate two simultaneous levels. On one level, they read a strange account of an otherworldly battle in the heavenly places, a story quite literally out of this world. On another level, though, they kept running into various details that had a distinct this-worldly ring. The images of "fleeing into the wilderness" and of "the male child who is to rule all the nations" are drawn from their every-Sunday liturgy, from often-told stories of Israel and Jesus. They would see their own faces among "those who keep the commandments of God and bear testimony to Jesus." That is characteristic Johannine language for obedient followers of Christ, and it was no stretch for them to discern their own sufferings in the warfare waged by the dying dragon on "the rest of her offspring." In other words, the text invited the readers to view their historical circumstances in the light of God's great victory, already announced with hymns of thanksgiving, in a world above historical time. Likewise, they were invited to see the great victory of God in the light of their pain-filled historical struggle to keep the commandments and bear witness to Christ.

3. I have already pointed to something of the *social context* of the first readers of Revelation. We do not know many precise details about the circumstances of the original readers, but we do know for certain that they were in trouble. Moreover, we know that their troubles were severe. Tribulation, poverty, suffering, the hour of trial — these are but a few of the distressful terms used to describe their situation. Some were threatened with imprisonment; others had been killed for their faith. There were dangers from without, and these were creating schisms within. Most commentators are persuaded that the recipients of Revelation were Christians under attack from the state, subject to forces to which which they were utterly powerless to respond in a political sense. The social system into which the book of Revelation was thrust was a world of a troubled prophetic, suffering community of Christians completely lacking in the strength to control their historical fate.

Now that we have explored the literary, generic, and social contexts of our text, we are ready to make a stab at describing how it functioned, as "performative language," for the reader. The situation is this: the Johannine community is under severe duress, and the writer of Revelation wishes to provide a resource for their troubled circumstances. Another writer in a different setting might have chosen political rhetoric (perhaps, "Make a difference! Register to vote," or even "Take up arms against the oppressor!"), psychological advice ("Let your problems be the occasion for personal growth"), or moral exhortation ("Stand up and be counted!"). Such strategies would be suitable only if the problems could be resolved with the political, personal, or moral resources at hand, however, and the first readers of Revelation had no such resources. They were being imprisoned and killed, and there was nothing whatsoever they could do about it. They were not up against some minor-league corruption in the county government or upset by some ripple on the surface of the psyche. They were facing some mauling, devouring, utterly destroying beast hungry for their blood, and to counsel them to adjust to the circumstances would have been to offer cruel comfort indeed.

In circumstances that dire, the Christian faith speaks in an apocalyptic voice; to silence that voice in such circumstances is to render the faith mute. The writer of Revelation chose the apocalyptic mode precisely because it is equipped to provide comfort, encouragement, and exhortation to people who are in situations that are not going to get better, that will not yield to any strategy for improvement. Like all other examples of the apocalyptic genre, Revelation 12 blends references to two worlds — the world of present history and the world beyond all time — and forges a metaphorical connection between the two. In this way it puts the crushing historical crisis into transhistorical perspective and "projects a definitive resolution" — not from the resources at hand but in the rule of God beyond all human grasping and manipulation.[12]

An event of suffering is composed of two main parts. First there is the infliction of pain, and second there is the response to that pain, the way in which the sufferer situates the pain in a network of meaning and potential counteraction. The former is a social action; the latter is an act of the imagination. Apocalyptic literature does not change the social circumstances; it does not make the pain go away. Rather, it seeks to change the response to that pain by shaping "one's imaginative perception" of it.[13] When suffering is so malicious and intense that no meaningful interpretation can be found for it in any available context, the startling language of Christian apocalyptic literature serves to draw back the curtains on a reality that cannot be seen by those who look only at the historical possibilities. The language of Revelation seeks not simply to communicate the fact but also to create the renewed conviction that Christ himself is "in the midst of the struggle, with and for the sake of his church. . . . In spite of it all, against it all, above it all, Jesus Christ is Lord."[14]

Preaching in an Apocalyptic Voice

We have explored how an apocalyptic text such as Revelation 12 employs its strange images and exotic language to create comfort and encouragement for a severely distressed Christian community. Is it possible for a contemporary preacher to produce a sermon on an apocalyptic text that

---

12. Collins, *The Apocalyptic Imagination*, p. 32.
13. Collins, *The Apocalyptic Imagination*, p. 32.
14. Allan Boesak, *Comfort and Protest: The Apocalypse from a South African Perspective* (Philadelphia: Westminster Press, 1987), p. 35.

does and says for modern hearers what that text did and said for its first reader? What might be the sound of a present-day apocalyptic voice?

David Buttrick is one contemporary homiletician who has tossed that question around, and he is of the opinion that "we cannot reinstate an apocalyptic mindset" for contemporary hearers and that we must not "image our way into absurdity" with talk of "bedsheet angels" and "cloudy courts of heaven."[15] He does, however, recognize that the apocalyptic conviction of a new world-age is essential to Christian faith, and so, as he sees it, the basic problem for preaching "is how to declare an exalted Christ without spouting a language so blatantly mythological as to be incredible."[16]

Buttrick's solution is to translate apocalyptic metaphors into narrative metaphors. Instead of describing dragons and heavenly warfare, the preacher can "insist that in Jesus Christ there has been a change in the plot line of the human story."[17] He offers the following illustration:

> Some years ago there was a Broadway play performed on two stages within one theater. On the center stage, actors acted their parts, while on a small stage, a single actor played the part of the playwright writing the play. If the actors bumped or muffed their lines, the playwright would scribble new scenes to straighten them out. Once, during the second act, the playwright leaped onto center stage and himself played a role. Back and forth, writing and rewriting, the playwright moved until at last the play came to a fine, free, dancing curtain call. Such is Christian conviction, a conviction contained in the apocalyptic image of a second coming. In spite of all appearances, we now live in the forming of God's new age. Christ is risen, and thus a new age has been inaugurated. Even now the coming of God's glad, sure conclusion impinges on our days.[18]

What Buttrick has attempted to do is to tame the wild language of apocalyptic while retaining its basic two-world structure. He does this because his concern is for apologetics. Buttrick seeks to help preachers articulate the gospel to modern people, who measure time by appointment calendars and digital watches and who are not about to be frequent flyers

---

15. Buttrick, *Preaching Jesus Christ* (Philadelphia: Fortress Press, 1988), pp. 65-66.
16. Buttrick, *Preaching Jesus Christ*, p. 66.
17. Buttrick, *Preaching Jesus Christ*, p. 67.
18. Buttrick, *Preaching Jesus Christ*, p. 67.

through open portals in an apocalyptic heaven. On the one hand, then, he does not want preachers to become unglued from this contemporary context and to start ranting like Hal Lindsey, but, on the other hand, he is not content to see the gospel reduced to the possibilities present in the visible world at hand. He retains the eschatological convictions of the gospel but sheds the apocalyptic garments.

Something crucial is lost, however, in the translation of apocalyptic language to the domesticated vocabulary of plot and drama. The picture of an offstage God writing a hidden but finally prevailing script for the human story *explains* the basic worldview of apocalyptic, all right, but it does not fully *perform* the linguistic work of the apocalyptic genre. Apocalyptic symbols strain the bonds of ordinary language. They have no obvious referents in the world at hand and are designed explicitly to explode the boundaries of the imagination. It is true, of course, that ordinary people today do not speak in apocalyptic terms, but it is also true that people in the first century did not routinely speak that way either. Even in the Johannine community, no one ever looked up from a bowl of porridge and casually said, "I saw one like a son of man with hair like white wool and eyes like a flame of fire." Such language is bizarre to modern ears; it was also bizarre then.

Listen to how another contemporary preacher, Allan Boesak, a minister in the Dutch Reformed Mission of South Africa and an eloquent critic of apartheid, exposits a verse from our sample text, preserving and extending the apocalyptic impact: "Rejoice then, O heaven and you that dwell therein! But woe to you, O earth and sea, for the devil has come down to you in great wrath, because he knows that his time is short!" (Rev. 12:12).

The devil is conquered, we have seen it, but the struggle is not yet over. The battle is won in heaven, but it is yet to begin in all earnest on earth. Even as the church rejoices in the first victory, it prepares for difficult days ahead. The devil has come down "in great wrath" because he has lost, but also because he knows that his time is short. And precisely because his time is short he will do as much damage as he can.

How well do we know that! The South African government's time is up. That we know. We are seeing the beginning of the end. But that does not stop them. Still they invent new weapons, which they display with great pride at the Arms Fair in Brazil. Still they announce newer, more refined anti-riot equipment: instant barbed wire fences falling out of the back of a truck like deadly vomit out of the mouth of a dragon. Still they legislate new powers for the Minister for Law and Order to declare any area an "unrest area," which means an emergency area without officially declaring a state of emergency. But oppressed people know what that means: the respectability of "law" for wanton destruction, unending streams of arrests, besieged townships, invaded communities and homes, fear-ridden streets, thousands of policemen and soldiers, grim and wild-eyed as they feverishly grip their guns — in a word, legalized murder. Indeed, how well John knows it. Woe! Oy! Prepare yourself, for he knows his time is short. But then again, rejoice! For we know it too.[19]

The important thing to note about this passage from Boesak is how the apocalyptic imagery of the text works powerfully, and without translation into other, less-fantastic terms, to interpret the contemporary situation. It even evokes from the contemporary side matching apocalyptic-sounding language: barbed wire fences falling "like deadly vomit out of the mouth of a dragon" and "grim, wild-eyed, feverish" soldiers and police.

The difference between Buttrick and Boesak, of course, is that Boesak is speaking both from and to a situation of social duress tragically similar to that of the first readers of Revelation.[20] But that, after all, is the point. In such situations, circumstances in which faithful people are for the foreseeable future powerless to overcome the evil surrounding and destroying them, the language of apocalyptic conveys the promises of the gospel in ways that no other, less dramatic idiom can perform. Boesak has given us a trenchant example of this.

The value of Buttrick's position, however, is that he has taken into account the fact that much preaching is to people who are not utterly powerless and who do have constructive options of exercising control. The proclamation of the hidden new age in Christ faithfully reminds such people "that the world is not controlled by the Caspar Weinbergers, or the KGBs, or even amiable, old, dangerous American presidents,"[21] thus

---

19. Boesak, *Comfort and Protest*, p. 90.

20. Paul Minear rejects the idea that apocalyptic literature can be successfully interpreted by a neutral interpreter. A modern exegete of apocalyptic materials, in Minear's view, must not only *believe* certain things (e.g., in a God who is working out the divine purpose; in creation as a whole) but must also be *situated* in a community of faith experiencing conflict (*New Testament Apocalyptic* [Nashville: Abingdon Press, 1981], p. 31).

21. Buttrick, *Preaching Jesus Christ*, p. 66.

freeing them for responsible obedience to the hidden reign of Christ. Indeed, to preach in an untranslated apocalyptic voice to Christians who retain some actual power in society is to risk irrelevance at best and to encourage faithless passivity at worst.

That is not to say, though, that there is no place for the unrestrained apocalyptic voice in preaching outside of South Africa and the barrio. In the first place, it is possible — actually essential — for Christians in places of relative calm to experience oneness with Christians under duress. The Christians to whom Allan Boesak speaks and the members of the First Suburban Church in Topeka belong to each other, and the story of the suffering saints in South Africa can be told in such a way that the apocalyptic gospel heard so directly and powerfully in Soweto can be overheard and celebrated in Kansas.

Moreover, there are regions of experience in every Christian community in which the beast makes war on powerless saints. What community of Christian people, even an ethically attuned one, does not detect beneath the usual array of "social problems" a destructive virulence, a greedy and devouring evil that no measure of responsible action can contain?

There is an astounding example of modern apocalyptic writing (dare we say *preaching?*) in Flannery O'Connor's short story "Revelation." The story involves a middle-aged farm woman, Mrs. Turpin, a southerner, who, along with her husband Claud and several other people, is seated in a doctor's waiting room. As the story unfolds, we are told of Mrs. Turpin's inner thoughts and we hear bits of her conversation with those in the room; through this we learn how she classifies various types of people in her world. On the bottom are most "colored people," though a few "clean, respectable" ones rise above the heap. Apart from them — "not above, just away from" — are the white trash. Above them are the home-owners; next come the home-and-land-owners (she and Claud are in this class); and finally there are "people with a lot of money and much bigger houses and much more land." This is not simply the world Mrs. Turpin sees; it is also the world Mrs. Turpin prefers and preserves with her thoughts and remarks. She believes, in fact, that this is the world Jesus intends for her to inhabit.

In the waiting room, a radio is softly playing gospel music, and Mrs. Turpin mentally sings along with the lyrics (and thus anticipates the apocalyptic denouement of the story): "When I looked up and He looked down . . . and wona these days I know I'll wear a crown." The turning point of the story comes when one of the people in the room, a silent and angry teenage girl, suddenly, and seemingly out of the blue, physically attacks Mrs. Turpin and says to her face, "Go back to hell where you came from, you old wart hog."

At one level, the girl's words are merely an angry curse, but at another level they are an apocalyptic revelation, and this, indeed, is how Mrs. Turpin hears them. She has not merely been insulted by a disturbed teenager; she has been named as the beast from hell by a messenger from God. Back at her farm, Mrs. Turpin cries out to the air — to God — "What do you send me a message like that for? . . . Who do you think you are?" She gazes up into the sky, and "a visionary light" settles in her eyes, revealing a vast swinging bridge extending from earth to heaven "through a field of living fire." A numberless company of souls is sweeping up this bridge toward heaven, whole companies of "white-trash," "colored," and "battalions of freaks and lunatics shouting and clapping and leaping like frogs." Bringing up the end of the procession is a tribe of people like herself and Claud, marching along as they lived, with great dignity, good order, and common sense. "Yet she could see by their shocked and altered faces that even their virtues were being burned away."

Mrs. Turpin turns from this vision to go down the path to the house, and the story closes with this sentence: "In the woods around her the invisible cricket choruses had struck up, but what she heard were the voices of the souls climbing upward into the starry field and shouting hallelujah."[22]

Through the vehicle of this short story, O'Connor releases the performative power of biblical apocalyptic language and symbols in such a way as to clarify the deadening structures of a particular society and to evoke the possibility of personal and social transformation. Preachers would do well to take note.

Or, again, for another example of the pertinence of apocalyptic imagery to the contemporary setting, listen to the detached voice of the *Encyclopaedia Britannica* as it describes the evil labor of cancer cells:

> If their growth is not checked, these cells infiltrate and destroy adjacent tissues. Often cancer cells are transported to distant parts of the body, where they grow as colonies called matastases. The cancerous or malig-

---

22. O'Connor, "Revelation," in *The Complete Stories of Flannery O'Connor* (New York: Farrar, Straus & Giroux, 1971), p. 509.

nant process begins as a progressive, unrestrained division of abnormal cells. . . . Some cancer cells may perform limited normal functions. As the disease progresses, however, the cells usually become increasingly abnormal in appearance, structure, and function until they may not be recognizable. . . . Chromosomes in malignant cells may appear oversized or may have asymmetrical spindles or other abnormalities.[23]

Even the clinical intent of that paragraph cannot avoid apocalyptic-style metaphors in describing the diabolic power of cancer. Cancer cells "infiltrate" and "destroy." They are viciously "malignant," but they may hide their malevolence behind the mask of "normality," crouching until the moment that they reveal their true shape as wrathful and sinister giants with "asymmetrical spindles."

Those who worship and serve the God of the Living have seen this beast before, for it has many manifestations. They have seen it in the oppressive tyrants of human history. They have seen it in Nero and in Hitler and in the bureaucratic administrators of apartheid. And now they see it yet again, this time slithering through the human body. Powerless before it, they nevertheless stand faithful, even as they are slain, clinging to the promise that the beast does not own the future, that Death and Hades will be thrown into the lake of fire, that God will wipe away every tear, and suffering and pain will be no more.

23. *Encyclopaedia Britannica*, 15th ed., s.v. "cancer."

Oral Methods of Structuring
Narrative in Mark

Joanna Dewey

In recent decades, scholars such as Walter Ong and Eric Havelock have developed an understanding of differences in oral and written composition and hermeneutics.[1] Werner Kelber in his seminal work *The Oral and the Written Gospel* has applied this knowledge to early Christian development. He argues persuasively for the significance of the shift from oral to written media for early Christianity, stressing the radical discontinuity between the two media. He sees in the Gospel of Mark a disruption of the oral synthesis, a new textuality arising "out of the debris of deconstructed orality."[2] While in no way questioning the importance of the medium shift for early Christianity, I will argue in this essay that the Gospel of Mark *as a whole* — not just its individual episodes — shows the legacy of orality, and indeed that its methods of composition are primarily oral.[3]

---

1. See, e.g., Ong, *The Presence of the Word: Some Prolegomena for Cultural and Religious History* (Minneapolis: University of Minnesota Press, 1967); *Interfaces of the Word: Studies in the Evolution of Consciousness and Culture* (Ithaca, N.Y.: Cornell University Press, 1977); and *Orality and Literacy: The Technologizing of the Word* (New York: Methuen, 1982); and Havelock, *Preface to Plato* (Cambridge: Harvard University Press, 1963); "The Oral and the Written Word: A Reappraisal," in *The Literate Revolution in Greece and Its Cultural Consequences* (Princeton: Princeton University Press, 1982), pp. 3-38; and "Oral Composition in the *Oedipus Tyrannus* of Sophocles," *New Literature History* 16 (1984): 175-97.

2. Kelber, *The Oral and the Written Gospel: The Hermeneutics of Speaking and Writing in the Synoptic Tradition, Mark, Paul, and Q* (Philadelphia: Fortress Press, 1983), p. 95.

3. Kelber makes his case on the basis of individual episodes rather than the Gospel as a whole (*The Oral and the Written Gospel*, pp. 44-89).

I

Before turning to the analysis of Mark, a few preliminary observations are in order. Kelber has emphasized the discontinuity between oral and written media. Yet, in a manuscript culture with high residual orality, there is considerable overlap between orality and textuality. First, the Gospel was *heard:* its reception remained aural. Thus oral techniques of composition are to be expected in the Gospel even if it was composed in writing. It had to be structured so that a listening audience could follow it. Walter Ong notes that even as late as the Renaissance, the listening audience had to be kept in mind while writing, citing the instance of an author revising an unsuccessful work "to make it more episodic and thus better fitted for oral reading to groups."[4] The needs of a listening audience would have been even more central in the first century in the social milieu of early Christianity.

Second, while an author may compose in writing, he or she can still draw on some techniques from the oral medium. Oral techniques continue to influence writing.[5] Ong states the principle that "a new technology of the word reinforces the old while at the same time transforming it."[6] At first writing was basically a transcription of oral performing, since no other compositional methods were yet known. In this context, writing tended to exaggerate oral techniques, employing even more *topoi* or creating even more extensive and elaborate structural patterns, since writing enabled a composer to do better what he or she was already doing. Only very gradually did techniques proper to the new medium take over.[7] On these grounds also, oral compositional techniques are to be expected in Mark.

So, assuming the Gospel of Mark to have been composed in writing, one would still expect it to have oral characteristics. Clearly the presence

---

4. Ong, *Orality and Literacy,* p. 158.

5. The reverse is also true: oral composers will come gradually to use some techniques first developed in writing. According to Ong, a somewhat more orderly linear account becomes possible, even demanded, in oral composition after it has been developed and assimilated through writing (*Interfaces of the Word,* p. 87). Further, oral lives may begin to present a single continuous story of a hero's life and death if this is the standard for written lives, even though, as Albert B. Lord points out, such comprehensive lives are not generally found in primary oral cultures ("The Gospels as Oral Traditional Literature," in *The Relationships among the Gospels: An Interdisciplinary Dialogue,* ed. William O. Walker Jr. [San Antonio: Trinity University, 1978], pp. 39-40).

6. Ong, *Orality and Literacy,* p. 153.

7. Ong, *Interfaces of the Word,* pp. 61-62; *Presence of the Word,* pp. 239-40.

of oral compositional devices would not prove that Mark was orally composed. It would indicate, however, that we should take oral hermeneutics into account in attempts to understand the Gospel.[8] I want to look at Mark with any eye on the structural characteristics of oral narrative as described primarily by Havelock, the foremost student of the shift from oral to written media in Greek cultures. My aim is to show that oral compositional techniques pervade the larger Gospel narrative and to trace out a few of the implications of this compositional status for understanding and preaching the Gospel.

II

In his *Preface to Plato,* Havelock argues persuasively that Plato's attack on poetry or mimesis in the *Republic* is in fact an attack on the whole oral mind-set of fourth-century Athens. According to Havelock, what Plato rejects about mimesis is what is characteristic of oral media. So, one way to approach the issue of oral structuring techniques in Mark is to compare the Gospel to Plato's understanding of mimesis. If Mark shares the characteristics of mimesis rejected by Plato, then the Gospel also shares characteristics of oral media. I shall first summarize Plato's description of mimesis (as interpreted by Havelock) and then analyze Mark with that in mind.

Plato held that poetry or mimesis includes far more than what we understand as poetry. He includes within this category — and rejects — not only poetic style but the entire content of epic and drama, the performer's identification with the content, his or her appeals to the audience's emotions, and the audience's identification with the performance.[9] Plato considers the content of mimesis to be merely *doxa,* or opinion, which,

8. A major reason for Kelber's rejection of oral hermeneutics for Mark is the Gospel's focus on Jesus' death in contrast to the oral emphasis on life and presence (*The Oral and the Written Gospel,* pp. 184-211). Yet the *Iliad* shows that a central concern with death is quite possible in oral media.

9. Havelock, *Preface to Plato,* pp. 20-35. Of course, Mark does not appear in elegant hexameters. But poetic meter is not central to Plato's argument against mimesis, which relates more to content and to the fact of oral performance. Furthermore, most oral poetry (apart from the Greek) had much simpler and freer rhythms, and oral prose narratives exist in many cultures (p. 130n.13). For a discussion of the difficulty of distinguishing prose and poetry in oral literature, see Ruth Finnegan, *Oral Poetry: Its Nature, Significance and Social Context* (Cambridge: Cambridge University Press, 1979), pp. 24-28.

he says, has three limitations: it is made up of happenings *(gignomena),* as
opposed to abstract thought; the happenings are visually concrete *(horata);*
and they are the many *(polla)* — that is, pluralized, not organized according to cause and effect.[10] For Plato, then, mimesis is only "an illusion of
reality" and "a phantom of virtue," the "stark antithesis" of knowledge or
science *(epistēmē);* it is utterly "alien" to thinking *(phrōnēsis).*[11]

Doxa Consists of Happenings

Plato's description of *doxa* fits the Gospel of Mark well. Mark certainly
consists of "happenings," "events in time," "episodes," "little stories or
situations."[12] "Information or prescription, which in a later stage of literate
culture would be arranged typically and topically," says Havelock, "is in
the oral tradition preserved only as it is transmuted into an event."[13] The
embedding of teaching in event is characteristic of Mark. For example,
unlike Matthew 6, with its general instructions on fasting and prayer, Mark
includes such teaching only in the context of events — the dispute over
why Jesus' disciples do not fast (2:18-20), and the episode of the discovery
of the withered fig tree (11:20-25).

Mark 4 and 13 may stretch the limits of oral memory's ability to
preserve instruction apart from event, although chapter 4 consists of
parables, little stories that can be remembered. Further, there is evidence
that the composer of chapter 4 had some difficulty in handling it. The
chapter begins with Jesus teaching the crowd from a boat on the lake
(4:1-2a), shifts to private discourse to explain the parable of the seed and
the sower (4:10), and then ends with Jesus still teaching the crowd from
the boat, without any transition (4:33-36). Listening audiences, which
cannot look back to earlier passages, tend to be more tolerant — or less
aware — of such lapses.

Mark 13, the apocalyptic discourse, does not consist of parables,
but it is largely narrative (albeit narrative of future events), and, as Jan
Lambrecht has shown, it is intricately patterned with much chiasm, ring

10. Havelock, *Preface to Plato,* p. 180.
11. Havelock, *Preface to Plato,* pp. 238-39.
12. Havelock, *Preface to Plato,* pp. 174, 180.
13. Havelock, *Preface to Plato,* p. 174. I note in passing that it may be the
difficulty of remembering sayings material apart from events that accounts for the early
writing of Q.

composition, and verbal echoing, all oral techniques designed to facilitate memory.[14] Twice the real audience is addressed — in verse 14 ("let the reader understand") and in verse 37 ("what I say to you I say to all: Watch"). We know from contemporary study that oral performers often make direct addresses to their live audiences.[15] Scholars have generally assumed that "reader" refers to the person reading Mark's Gospel, who is being encouraged to understand the reference to Daniel's "abomination of desolation" correctly.[16] This interpretation is difficult to sustain, however, since the Gospel was hardly designed for or likely to appeal to the limited first-century reading public. I contend that the "reader" here is not the reader of Mark but the reader of Daniel. Bultmann also suggests this possibility, noting that the words "to read" and "reading" are used particularly for public reading in the synagogue or congregation.[17] Thus Mark's use of "reader" in verse 14 is not a stumbling block to an oral understanding of the Gospel. The second aside, "what I say to you I say to all," serves to extend the teaching embedded in the event from the four disciples who are part of the episode to apply to the listening audience. Teaching in Mark is conveyed through events or happenings.

Doxa Consists of the Visible

Oral compositions will be more readily remembered if their episodes are visual — that is, if they can be pictured in the mind's eye. Havelock writes, "In their separate and episodic independence from each other they are visualized sharply, passing along in an endless panorama."[18] The episodes in Mark are easily visualized. This is clearly true of individual units with much concrete detail, such as the healing of the paralytic and the flight

14. Lambrecht, "La structure de Mc., XIII," in *De Jésus aux Evangiles,* ed. I. de La Potterie, BETL, vol. 25, no. 2 (Gembloux: Editions J. Duculot, 1967), pp. 141-64.

15. See, e.g., Ilhan Basgöz, "The Tale-Singer and His Audience," in *Folklore: Performance and Communication,* ed. Dan Ben-Amos and Kenneth S. Goldstein (The Hague: Mouton Publishers, 1975), pp. 143-203.

16. See, e.g., Vincent Taylor, *The Gospel according to St. Mark,* 2d ed. (London: Macmillan, 1966), pp. 511-12; and William L. Lane, *Commentary on the Gospel of Mark,* NICNT (Grand Rapids: William B. Eerdmans, 1974), p. 467.

17. Bultmann, "ἀγανινώσκω, ἀνάγνωσις," in *Theological Dictionary of the New Testament,* vol. 1, ed. Gerhard Kittel and Gerhard Friedrich, trans. Geoffrey W. Bromiley (Grand Rapids: William B. Eerdmans, 1964), pp. 343-44.

18. Havelock, *Preface to Plato,* p. 180.

of the demons into the pigs, pericopes that clearly had a prior existence in oral tradition. But it is also true of the summary statements, K. L. Schmidt's *Sammelberichte,* which are generally assumed to be Mark's own written contribution.[19] We tend to think of such passages as less colorful and as different in kind, yet when we hear them as part of a succession of incidents, they are easily visualized. For example, Mark 2:13 ("He went out again beside the sea; and all the crowd gathered about him, and he taught them") suggests a vignette of Jesus addressing a crowd on rather barren ground against a background of blue water. The general healing passages such as Mark 3:7-12 and 6:53-56 can be visualized as crowd scenes with people jostling about and pushing to get their sick to Jesus. To draw an analogy from film, the effect is that of drawing back for a distant shot between sequences of closeups. When one hears the Gospel, the passages do not seem set off in kind; they, too, are "visibles."[20]

Doxa Consists of the Many

Plato's third complaint about opinion is that it is made up of the many, not the one. Ong describes this feature as the additive and aggregative character of oral narrative.[21] To illustrate the difference, Ong contrasts the Douay version (1610) of the opening of Genesis, which preserves the additive style of the Hebrew, with the New American Bible (1970), a more contemporary translation:

Douay: In the beginning God created heaven, and earth. And the earth was void and empty, and darkness was upon the face of the deep; and the spirit of God moved over the waters. And God said: Be light made. And light was made. And God saw the light that it was good; and he divided the light from the darkness. And he called the light Day, and the darkness Night; and there was evening and morning one day.

New American: In the beginning, when God created the heavens and the earth, the earth was a formless wasteland, and darkness covered

---

19. See, e.g., Kelber, *The Oral and the Written Gospel,* p. 51.
20. The fact that the summary statements function as scenes becomes quite clear as one watches David Rhoads's videotape *Dramatic Performance of Mark* (Columbus: Select, 1985).
21. Ong, *Orality and Literacy,* pp. 37-39.

the abyss, while a mighty wind swept over the waters. Then God said, "Let there be light," and there was light. God saw how good the light was. God then separated the light from the darkness. God called the light "day" and the darkness he called "night." Thus evening came, and morning followed — the first day.

In place of the nine introductory *and*'s of the Douay/Hebrew, the modern translation has only two *and*'s and a *when,* a *while,* a *thus,* and two *then*'s. With our sensibilities formed in a print culture, we read analytic relationships into the additive oral narrative.

In oral narrative, *and* links not only clauses and sentences but also whole pericopes. Havelock writes that the oral tradition is

> remembered and frozen into the record as separate disjunct episodes each complete and satisfying in itself, in a series which is joined together paratactically. Action succeeds action in a kind of endless chain. The basic grammatical expression which would symbolise the link of event to event would be simply the phase "and next. . . ."[22]

The Markan narrative is clearly a series of independent episodes joined by *and.* Of the thirteen pericope introductions in Mark 1–2, eleven begin with *kai.*[23] Only Mark 1:1, the opening of the Gospel, and 1:14, the beginning of Jesus' public ministry, do not.[24]

Furthermore, the sequence of paratactic episodes is generally not determined by attaching subordinate to main acts or by connecting cause and effect.[25] "One of the places where oral mnemonic structures and procedures manifest themselves most spectacularly is in their effect on narrative plot," writes Ong, "which in an oral culture is not quite what we take plot typically to be," for it makes no attempt at climactic linear development.[26]

Certainly there is no attempt in Mark to develop a gradually intensifying conflict between Jesus and the authorities, rising to a climax at the arrest and crucifixion. The hostility first rises to a climax in 3:6, where the Pharisees and Herodians plot to kill Jesus. It is then forgotten about

---

22. Havelock, *Preface to Plato,* p. 180.

23. See the English titles in the United Bible Societies' Greek text.

24. Here also, modern versions tend to reduce sharply the number of *and*'s. The relatively literal RSV keeps six of the eleven *and*'s in Mark 1–2; the NEB keeps none.

25. Havelock, *Preface to Plato,* pp. 182-83.

26. Ong, *Orality and Literacy,* pp. 141, 142-43.

for eight chapters (although there are occasional conflicts between Jesus and the authorities) until, in 11:18 and 12:12, the authorities, the chief priests, elders, and scribes, seek to kill Jesus. The level of conflict then appears to decrease in the remaining controversies in Mark 12, ending with a scribe and Jesus praising each other in 12:32-34. But then in 14:1 the authorities again seek Jesus' life, and the actual plot to arrest him is finally set in motion. Contemporary Markan scholars, long accustomed to the linearity typical of print narrative, have tended to attribute Mark's order (or lack of order) either to his "simple" writing style or to his incorporation of sources. In all probability, it is the natural consequence of his oral narrative technique.

If the episodes in oral narrative are not grouped according to cause and effect (i.e., in linear plot development), neither are they necessarily arranged in chronological order. "The poet will report a situation and only much later explain, often in detail, how it came to be."[27] The past is brought into the narrative only at the point at which it becomes relevant to some episode being narrated.[28] Thus, in Mark, the details of John the Baptist's arrest and death appear not in the first chapter, where John's arrest is noted in verse 14, but in chapter 6, in connection with the explanation of why Herod might have suspected that Jesus was John raised from the dead. Here again the Markan narrative follows oral ordering principles. It is made up of the many; it does not subordinate the many to the one.

Thus, Mark may be said to consist of *doxa*. The narrative consists of events that are visible and made up of many. It is not ordered logically in terms of time, as those accustomed to print expect. As *doxa*, its contents and the way they are ordered are typical of oral narrative.

III

Not only does Mark conform to the limitations of *doxa*, but the Gospel's methods of narrative development also correspond to those found in oral compositions. As Havelock puts it, "The basic principle . . . can be stated abstractly as variation within the same."[29] Oral narrative "operates on

27. Ong, *Orality and Literacy*, p. 142.
28. See Havelock, *Preface to Plato*, p. 179.
29. Havelock, *Preface to Plato*, p. 147.

the acoustic principle of the echo."[30] Ring composition *(inclusio)* is endemic in oral narrative, marking the boundaries of individual episodes and of much longer sections. Ong notes that individual episodes and clusters of episodes are narrated in balanced patterns in either parallel or chiastic order.[31] Havelock comments that when we notice these correspondences at all, we tend to call them "patterns" — a visual concept; he suggests that it would be more appropriate to think of them as acoustic responses.[32]

Scholars have been noticing patterns — or acoustic responses — in Mark for some time now. The Markan sandwiches are a form of ring composition. Scholars have suggested more elaborate concentric or parallel rhythms for several sections of Mark, among them 1:16-45; 2:1–3:6; 4:1-34; 8:27–9:13; 12:1-40; and 13:5b-37.[33] (It should be noted that these sections are relatively brief, covering five or six pericopes, a length during which an oral performer can easily manipulate both structural and verbal parallels. Even in writing, Mark is still conforming to the restrictions on oral composition.) Although the proposed structures are not all equally convincing, the very fact they can be posited is an indication of the quantity of thematic and verbal echoes to be found in the Gospel.

The longer narrative is also formulated on acoustic response. Ong speaks of oral narrative as episodes strung "together in . . . intricately managed patterns."[34] Havelock spells out the oral narrative chaining method in more detail:

> The same compositional principle [the echo principle] extends itself to the construction of the tale as a whole; it will avoid sheer surprise and novel invention. . . . The basic method for assisting the memory to retain a series of distinct meanings is to frame the first of them in a way which will suggest or forecast a later meaning which will recall the first without being identical with it. What is to be said and remembered later is cast in the form of an echo of something said already; the future is encoded in the present. All oral narrative is in

30. Havelock, "Oral Composition," p. 182.

31. Ong, *Orality and Literacy*, p. 34.

32. Havelock, "Oral Composition," p. 183.

33. See Joanna Dewey, *Markan Public Debate: Literary Technique, Concentric Structure, and Theology in Mark 2:1–3:6*, SBLDS, vol. 48 (Chico, Cal.: Scholars Press, 1980), p. 144. See also Benôit Standaert, *L'Évangile selon Marc: Composition et genere littéraire* (Zevenkerken: Brugge, 1978), pp. 174-262.

34. Ong, *Interfaces of the Word*, p. 284.

structure continually both prophetic and retrospective. . . . Though
the narrative syntax is paratactic — the basic conjunction being "and
then," "and next" — the narrative is not linear but turns back on itself
in order to assist the memory to reach the end by having it anticipated
somehow in the beginning.[35]

Such a description applies remarkably well to the Markan narrative.
Norman Petersen has pointed to numerous prospective and retrospective
references in Mark as evidence that the narrative was deliberately plotted.[36]
It also would seem to be evidence that the plotting of the narrative employs
typical oral techniques. The material is not ordered logically or chrono-
logically but rather by anticipation and responsion, so that what is new is
framed in terms of what is already known.

The plethora of backward and forward echoes that constitute the
narrative of Mark become more evident (to us) if we consider those places
where scholars have posited breaks in Mark's outline. Scholars have failed
to reach consensus on the exact outline or structure of Mark, though not
for lack of trying. I have argued that this is because Mark does not have
a single linear structure; rather the structure consists of overlapping
repetitive sequences.[37] All portions of Mark where scholars frequently
place breaks (i.e., chaps. 1, 3, 8, 10–11, and 14) actually participate in
several different overlapping sequences, echoing both backward and forward in the narrative. I shall use Mark 8 as an example of these multiple
echoes, of variation within repetition, since virtually every scholar posits
a major new beginning at either 8:22 (the story of the blind man of
Bethsaida) or 8:27 (the account of Peter's recognition of Jesus as the
Christ).

The Echo System in Mark 8

It has become commonplace to view the healing at Bethsaida in 8:22-26
along with the healing of blind Bartimaeus at Jericho in 10:46-52 as a

35. Havelock, "Oral Composition," p. 183.
36. Petersen, *Literary Criticism for New Testament Critics* (Philadelphia: Fortress
Press, 1978), pp. 49-80.
37. Dewey, "Mark's Structure: Discrete Segments or Interwoven Tapestry?" (paper
presented at the annual meeting of the Catholic Biblical Association, San Francisco, August
1985).

frame to the "way section" in which Jesus teaches about the way of the cross,[38] and quite properly so. They are the only healings of blindness in the Gospel.[39] The pericopes begin identically: "And they are going to Bethsaida/Jericho" (8:22; 10:46).[40] Bethsaida and Jericho are near the northern and southern points of Jesus' journey to Jerusalem. Significantly, the Bethsaida healing is accomplished in two stages, suggesting that the following teaching is difficult, whereas the Jericho healing is instantaneous and Bartimaeus follows Jesus on the way. So the healing at Bethsaida does point ahead in the narrative, or, in Havelock's terms, the Bartimaeus healing is an echo and variation on the Bethsaida healing.

Yet for the person listening to Mark, the most obvious thing about the blind man of the Bethsaida story is not its newness, pointing ahead, but its retrospective echo of the healing of the deaf and dumb man in 7:31-37. Both begin "And they [some people] brought to him . . . and they besought [begged] him to . . ." (7:32; 8:22). Both are healings by physical means using spittle (the only such healings in Mark). And the verbal echoes are extensive throughout.[41] Indeed, the similarities are such that Bultmann considered them to be two versions of the same episode.[42] The hearers are hardly likely to miss the echo.[43]

After the healing at Bethsaida, the next reported healing in Mark — that of the boy with the unclean spirit (9:14-27) — echoes both the Bethsaida and the deaf-mute healing (and also earlier exorcisms). The healing of the unclean boy and the healing at Bethsaida are both done in two stages. In neither does the restored person or the watching crowd do anything as the result of the healing; but the boy's unclean spirit is not

---

38. See, e.g., Norman Perrin and Dennis C. Duling, *The New Testament: An Introduction,* 2d ed. (New York: Harcourt Brace Jovanovich, 1982), pp. 248-49.

39. The term *typhlos* occurs twice in the Bethsaida story, three times in the Bartimaeus story, and nowhere else in Mark.

40. While pericopes beginning with Jesus coming or going somewhere are common, the only other instances of *erchomai eis* in a pericope introduction are found in 3:20 *(kai erchetai eis oikon)* and 11:27 *(kai erchontai palin eis Ierosolyma). Kai ēlthon eis* also occurs twice (5:1; 9:33).

41. A convenient comparison of the Greek can be found in Taylor, *The Gospel according to St. Mark,* pp. 368-69.

42. Bultmann, *The History of the Synoptic Tradition,* trans. John Marsh (New York: Harper & Row, 1963), p. 213.

43. Albert Lord, the oral critic par excellence, who concluded that the Synoptic Gospels are oral variants, was particularly struck by the presence of doublets in the Gospels as evidence for their oral composition ("The Gospels as Oral Traditional Literature," p. 76).

one of blindness but rather deafness and dumbness, which harks back to the deaf-mute healing in Mark 7.[44]

In addition, the third healing, the one of the boy with the unclean spirit, anticipates the final healing, that of blind Bartimaeus. These two healings are accomplished by a spoken word, not by physical action as the earlier two are; and both involve faith.[45] Finally, the Bartimaeus healing echoes the first, the deaf-mute healing, in that both involve responses in which someone disobeys Jesus' command: in Mark 7:36, "they" were commanded to silence but preached all the more; in Mark 10:52, Bartimaeus was commanded to depart but immediately followed Jesus on the way. Thus these four healings ring the changes on restoring hearing, speech, and sight. Here there is certainly the sort of variety within repetition that is characteristic of oral narrative, without any definite starting or ending point.

Similarly, the second passage considered a major new beginning in Mark 8, Peter's recognition of Jesus as the Christ, echoes backward and forward in the narrative. The verses climax the preceding eight chapters: the disciples finally recognize who Jesus is, something the hearer was told in Mark 1:1. They begin the "way" section, which runs to the Bartimaeus healing. They lead immediately into the first passion prediction, which obviously anticipates the second and third predictions.

Yet for the listener, their most obvious feature would be their echo of Mark 6:14-16, in which Herod decides that Jesus is John the Baptist raised from the dead. Not only are most of the suggestions about who Jesus is the same, but the structural sequence of the two passages is similar. (Structural sequence is, of course, the basis of oral memory.) First, each lists the possibilities for who Jesus is: in 6:14-15, "John the baptizer," "Elijah," and "a prophet, like one of the prophets of old"; in 8:28, "John the Baptist," "Elijah," and "one of the prophets." Second, in each passage someone recognizes Jesus: in Mark 6:16 Herod says, "John, whom I beheaded, has been raised"; in Mark 8:29 Peter says, "You are the Christ." Finally, there is the theme of death: Herod's execution of John the Baptist in 6:17-29, and the prediction that the Son of Humanity will be killed in 8:31.

---

44. 7:32, *kōphon kai mogilalon;* 7:37, *tous kōphous poiei akouein kai alalous lalein;* 9:17, *pneuma alalon;* 9:25, *to alalon kai kōphon pneuma.* These are the only uses of *kōphos, alalos,* and *mogilalos* in Mark.

45. 9:24, *pisteuō boēthei mou tē apistia;* 10:52, *hē pistis sou sesōken se.*

As in the healing of the blind man at Bethsaida, what leads forward in the narrative to new material is formulated as an echo of what has been said already. Mark certainly seems to have followed the oral method outlined by Havelock for the tale as a whole: the way to show a "series of distinct meanings is to frame the first of them in a way which will suggest or forecast a later meaning which will recall the first without being identical to it."[46] In summary, Mark indeed possesses Havelock's characteristics of oral narrative. It is made up of happenings that are easily visualized and that are arranged not in a logical order but in an endless chain of association based on the echo principle.

IV

The fact that the Gospel of Mark is marked by the characteristics of oral narrative suggests that it was composed for a listening rather than a reading audience. This suggests that we need to take the dynamics of orality much more seriously in interpreting the Gospel and in reconstructing early Christian history. A few suggestions for doing so follow.

The Negative Portrayal of the Disciples

As Ong has repeatedly stressed, oral narrative tends to be "agonistically toned" — that is, strongly polemic.[47] Accustomed to an adversarial atmosphere, a first-century audience hearing the Gospel would probably have taken the negative portrayal of the disciples much less seriously than contemporary Markan scholars do.[48] Instruction often was conveyed to an audience through "warning examples of how not to behave."[49] Achilles in the *Iliad* provides an excellent example of how not to behave to win a war (although Alexander the Great quite consciously took Achilles as his model as he campaigned to conquer the world). Also, to understand the role of the disciples, we need to

46. Havelock, "Oral Composition," p. 183.
47. Ong, *Orality and Literacy,* pp. 43-45; *Presence of the Word,* pp. 195-207.
48. See especially Theodore J. Weeden, *Mark-Traditions in Conflict* (Philadelphia: Fortress Press, 1971); and Kelber, *The Oral and the Written Gospel,* p. 186.
49. Havelock, *Preface to Plato,* p. 48.

consider the process of identification with the characters that occurs in oral performance.[50] The identification occurs in succession — that is, the performer and audience identify first with Jesus and then with the disciples.[51] Since oral narrative consists of the many not logically connected, it can tolerate different viewpoints in a way print culture cannot. As Ong rephrases Lévi-Strauss, "the oral mind totalizes" rather than analyzes.[52] Acceptance of Jesus need not mean rejection of the disciples. We need to rethink the question of the role of the disciples in Mark in light of oral processes. Perhaps we will reach greater agreement on their significance in the story.

The Open Ending of Mark

Several scholars have argued that the Gospel as a whole is a parable writ large.[53] The parable works best in an oral setting in which the performer, in interaction with the audience, can make sure the point of the parable is grasped — whether accepted or rejected. In the written tradition, parables became allegories and moral examples; they lost their parabolic force. Perhaps something similar happened with the Gospel of Mark. As long as the Gospel was performed orally, the open ending could function very well before a live audience. Yet when the Gospel came to be treated as a writing, its parabolic function was no longer understood, its open ending became ambiguous and intolerable, and the longer endings were felt to be necessary to provide a resolution.[54] We also need to rethink the Markan ending in light of oral processes.

50. See Havelock, *Preface to Plato,* pp. 44-45, 145-64.
51. Concerning reader identification with the disciples, see Robert C. Tannehill, "The Disciples in Mark: The Function of a Narrative Role," *Journal of Religion* 57 (1977): 386-405; and "The Gospel of Mark as Narrative Christology," *Semeia* 16 (1979): 57-95. Concerning reader identification with Jesus, see Norman Petersen, " 'Point of View' in Mark's Narrative," *Semeia* 12 (1978): 97-121; and Mary Ann Tolbert, "1978 Markan Seminar: Response to Robert Tannehill," Seminar on Mark, Society of Biblical Literature, 1978. For a literary argument that the reader identifies with both, see Joanna Dewey, "Point of View and the Disciples in Mark," *1982 Seminar Papers,* SBLASP, vol. 118 (1982): 97-106.
52. Ong, *Orality and Literacy,* p. 175.
53. See Kelber, *The Oral and the Written Gospel,* pp. 117-29, 215-20; Elizabeth Struthers Malbon, "Mark: Myth and Parable," *Biblical Theology Bulletin* 16 (1986): 8-17; and the literature they cite.
54. Several scholars have recently suggested that the ending at Mark 16:8 is a call to the reader to complete the narrative and follow Jesus. See, e.g., Norman Petersen, "When

Oral Narrative in the Early Church

I have argued that Mark was composed in writing for a listening audience. Yet the prevalence of oral compositional techniques suggests to me that we need to ask again if Mark is a written transcription of oral narrative or if — a more likely circumstance — Mark is building on an oral story-telling tradition.[55] The Gospel of Mark possesses both oral methods of connecting individual episodes and a very high degree of inner consistency among the episodes.[56] It seems more plausible to suppose that this structure is the result of Mark's having been built on an existing oral narrative tradition of some sort than to suppose that the disparate episodes of the synoptic tradition were connected for the first time in the written text. The form-critical assumption that there was no story of Jesus prior to the written Gospels, that there were only individual stories about Jesus, also needs to be reconsidered in the light of our growing knowledge of oral narrative.

First-Century Media Model

Finally, or perhaps first of all, we must develop a media model for the Gospel of Mark and early Christianity in general. We need a better understanding of how oral and written media worked both together and in opposition to each other in the early Christian mixed-media situation. I agree with Werner Kelber that we need to take into account the shift from oral to written media in understanding Christian development. The

---

Is the End Not the End? Literary Reflections on the Ending of Mark's Narrative," *Interpretation* 34 (1980): 151-66. Yet as Ong points out, writers have had to educate readers over time to participate appropriately in their writings ("The Writer's Audience Is Always a Fiction," in *Interfaces of the Word*, pp. 53-81). It is questionable whether a first-century *reader* would have been able to follow an ending such as 16:8.

55. Since Johann Gottfried Herder in the eighteenth century, Thorleif Boman, Albert B. Lord, and Thomas E. Boomershine have argued that Mark is an oral composition. For specific references, see Kelber, *The Oral and the Written Gospel*, pp. 77-78. For a summary of scholarship on early Christian storytellers, see Leander E. Keck, "Oral Traditional Literature and the Gospels: The Seminar," in *The Relationships among the Gospels*, pp. 108-13.

56. Concerning literary consistency in Mark, see David Rhoads and Donald Michie, *Mark as Story: An Introduction to the Narrative of a Gospel* (Philadelphia: Fortress Press, 1982), and the literature cited there.

Gospel of Mark (whether as written composition or as transcription of oral story) is only the first step in the transition to a written hermeneutic, a process that took decades if not centuries.

V

Implications and Cautions for Preaching

The Gospels were composed to be heard rather than read. Hearing — storytelling and listening — has power. Jesus' stories, the parables, called and empowered hearers to transform their lives. In the first century, the Gospels — stories *about* Jesus — called and empowered hearers to transform their lives. Today, our continued use and development of the biblical stories enable us to transform and empower our lives as Christians. We need to tap into the storytelling power, but we need also to be aware of the dangers. Let us use storytelling in preaching to empower, not to destroy or oppress.

1. *Tell the stories, don't read them.* In telling stories, we make them our own. They become part of our experience. "To become a teller of Jesus' tales is to become a disciple of Jesus. . . . The story journey means participating in Jesus' journey."[57] The Gospel stories can be told and heard in various ways. One way is to memorize them in a good modern translation (RSV, NEB, etc.) and retell them as translated. Thomas Boomershine's little book *Story Journey* is very helpful in explaining both why and how to learn to tell the Gospel stories as they were written and translated.[58] On occasion, the retelling by preachers or groups from the congregation of a portion of the biblical narrative that they have made their own can serve as an effective sermon.

Use imagination. It can be helpful not only to tell the story in the biblical words but to retell it in our own words. Shift the perspective of the story: retell it from the point of view of each of the different characters within it. Become not only the narrator but also in turn the Syrophoenician woman and Jesus (Mark 7:24-30), for example. Continue the story in your imagination: imagine you are the Syrophoenician woman's daughter from

---

57. Thomas E. Boomershine, *Story Journey: An Invitation to the Gospel as Storytelling* (Nashville: Abingdon Press, 1988), p. 197.

58. See also Richard L. Eslinger, *A New Hearing: Living Options in Homiletic Method* (Nashville: Abingdon Press, 1987).

whom the demon was cast out, or an adult woman telling her own children the story or preaching to a young struggling Christian congregation. A student gave an effective Easter sermon speaking from the perspective of an aged Mary Magdalene, commenting on the various Gospel stories about her. Encourage members of your congregation to use their imaginations in retelling and developing the stories in ways that transform and empower them.

It is true that in using our imaginations we run the risk of distorting the meanings. Careful exegetical work is always requisite. But imagination has already transformed/distorted the traditions in incorporating them into the Gospels. And we transform/distort them again simply by hearing and telling them in a twentieth-century First World context rather than in a Third World, colonized, first-century context.[59] To tell or hear a story is always to use our imaginations. Let us recognize that and use our imaginations intentionally, creatively, and responsibly.

2. *Beware of meaning as reference.* A story's meaning comes from its plot, not from its reference to historical events, however accurate or inaccurate that history may be.[60] For example, the Gospels *plot* Jesus' resurrection as good news, but the same event could equally be plotted as quite irrelevant, an oddity that happened once somewhere remote, of no consequence to anyone; or it could be plotted as bad news. Many in the Roman Empire believed that Nero would be resurrected and lead a triumphant army of barbarians against the Empire — an example of resurrection as tragedy.

We twentieth-century Americans have been trained from childhood up to understand meaning as reference, to understand the Gospels as meaningful only insofar as they describe exactly what happened at a particular time and place. Biblical literalism is alive and well in our culture. I believe it is very important in telling biblical stories, especially in telling them from the pulpit with the added authority that gives, to avoid reinforcing the common assumption that the story equals what actually happened on the roads of Galilee and Judea. Since we are trained to hear story as history, this involves constant reminders to the listening audience: "I imagine . . . ," "We don't, of course, know what Jesus actually said . . . ,"

59. For help in hearing Mark in something closer to its original context, see Herman C. Waetjen, *A Reordering of Power: A Socio-Political Reading of Mark's Gospel* (Minneapolis: Fortress Press, 1989); and Ched Myers, *Binding the Strong Man: A Political Reading of Mark's Story of Jesus* (Maryknoll, N.Y.: Orbis Books, 1988).

60. See Bruce J. Malina, *Christian Origins and Cultural Anthropology: Practical Models for Biblical Interpretation* (Atlanta: John Knox Press, 1986), pp. 166-84.

"The leper might have thought . . . ," and so forth. The explicit use of imagination — speaking from the persona of the Syrophoenician woman's daughter — can help a congregation both to hear the story's message and to distinguish it from a recital of historical facts.

3. *Beware of unwanted ideological baggage in a story.* Stories have power because, in hearing and telling them, we enter their narrative world, their versions of reality. This enables their versions of reality. We meet Jesus in the Gospel story and can be transformed by him. But we also meet a good deal else from first-century culture that we may not wish to be influenced by. The Gospel's narrative worlds present some special dangers, such as their marginalization of women and their potential to reinforce anti-Semitism.

The Bible was written in an androcentric and patriarchal culture, in which the male was the human norm and men were valued more than women. Retelling the Gospel narratives only in their own words would reinforce the androcentric and patriarchal aspects of our own culture. For example, Mark tells us some sixteen verses from the end of his Gospel that among those watching the crucifixion were women who had followed Jesus in Galilee and come up with him to Jerusalem — that is, there were women among the close disciples of Jesus, and they had been there all along. Since women were prominent in all aspects of the life of the early church,[61] in all probability the Gospel's original audiences were aware of this fact, and hence the imaginative picture they formulated of Jesus' disciples as they heard Mark's narrative would have included women as well as men. But we, hearing only the androcentric narrative, are at risk of formulating an imaginative picture of only men in the inner circle around Jesus, and the late mention of the women in Mark may barely make a dent in our imaginative reconstruction. The androcentric narrative reinforces continued discrimination against women in our churches and culture. If one believes that the marginalization and oppression of any individuals or groups is contrary to the liberating message of Christianity, then one must take active measures to counter the androcentric bias of the biblical narrative. We need to imagine the women back into the story.[62]

61. See Elisabeth Schüssler Fiorenza, *In Memory of Her: A Feminist Theological Reconstruction of Christian Origins* (New York: Crossroad, 1983), pp. 105-204.

62. Two particularly helpful resources are Sandra M. Schneiders's *Women and the Word: The Gender of God in the New Testament and the Spirituality of Women* (New York: Paulist Press, 1986) and Fiorenza's *In Memory of Her.*

The Gospels also serve to reinforce or even create anti-Semitism. By entering their narrative worlds, we are encouraged to view Jews as enemies.[63] The Markan Jesus, a Jew, criticizes the Jewish leaders, much as we American citizens are prone to criticize our elected representatives in Washington. But as the Gospels moved farther away from Jesus' Jewish context, the criticism of the leaders came to be heard and told as criticism of the Jewish people. The New Testament has been a major source for and legitimation of the persecution of Jews that has characterized much of Christian history. As we retell the biblical stories, we must actively counter the anti-Semitism that is part of the biblical story worlds.

The Gospels were powerful tools in the spread of Christianity in part because they were stories that were told and heard. We can tap into that power today by continuing to tell and hear the stories. But as we do, we need to use our critical suspicions and our imaginations so that we tell the stories in ways that are empowering for all people, for in Christ "there is neither Jew nor Greek, there is neither slave nor free, there is neither male nor female" (Gal. 3:28).

63. See Norman A. Beck, *Mature Christianity: The Recognition and Repudiation of the Anti-Jewish Polemic of the New Testament* (Selinsgrove, Pa.: Susquehanna University Press, 1985).

A Poetics of the Pulpit
for Post-Modern Times

Thomas H. Troeger

Poetics and Homiletics: An Awkward Marriage

The title of this essay will trouble many readers. The phrase "a poetics of the pulpit" may seem to imply a fancified preaching, more concerned with aesthetic values than theological truth. No preacher wants to bear the charge that John Wesley brought against the proclamations of James Wheatly: "an unconnected rhapsody of unmeaning words, like Sir John Suckling's — Verses, smooth and soft as cream, in which was neither depth nor stream."[1]

The awkwardness of joining homiletics and poetics reflects the history of the stormy relationship between religion and imagination. Meir Sternberg reflects the burden of past suspicions between the two in the opening of his book on the poetics of biblical narrative:

> To many, Poetics and Bible do not easily make a common household even as words. But I have deliberately joined them together, avoiding more harmonious terms like Structure or Shape or Art in order to leave no doubt about my argument. Poetics is the systematic working or study of literature as such. Hence, to offer a poetics of biblical narrative is to claim that biblical narrative is a work of literature.[2]

1. Wesley, "Letter on Preaching, Christ," 10 December 1751, in *Theories of Preaching: Selected Readings in the Homiletical Tradition,* ed. Richard Lischer (Durham, N.C.: Labyrinth Press, 1987), p. 109.
2. Sternberg, *The Poetics of Biblical Narrative* (Bloomington, Ind.: Indiana University Press, 1985), p. 2.

42

In a similar fashion, the conjunction of homiletics and poetics illuminates the implicit theories, values, and understandings of language that operate in our preaching. There *is* a poetics of the pulpit whether we are aware of it or not. As Phillips Brooks recognized over a century ago, "Preaching in every age follows, to a certain extent, the changes which come to all literature and life,"[3] and thus the pulpit for good and for ill gets entangled in the general poetics of the culture.

Although I will sometimes draw on poetics as "the systematic working or study of literature,"[4] I am using the term more precisely to mean *the character of our articulation of reality as it arises from our historically conditioned imaginative construction of the world.* For example, everything I have so far written reflects the fact that I teach in a theological school in the Northeastern United States and am writing to contribute to a collection of essays on the nature of homiletics in the late twentieth century. Each of these factors influences my choice of words and the way I put these words together — my poetics. I do not use the same poetics when I step into the pulpit. That is a different context, and it therefore changes the character of the way I articulate reality. In the pulpit I must express myself orally, but here I am writing material to be processed by the eye and the mind of you, the reader who has entered the "historically conditioned imaginative construction of the world" that informs this book through the peculiarities of its editor and authors.

Furthermore, I call the strategies of language that I am describing *a* — not *the* — poetics because my perspectives will not fit the theology of all readers. My poetics may in fact be most valuable to you at those points where you disagree with me, especially if, instead of building rational arguments against what is offered here, you analyze the material circumstances of your life that lead you to respond as you do.

The Material Foundation of Our Poetics

I began to write this essay after having two wisdom teeth out. When the anesthetic wore off, I felt as though a nail was being driven from my right ear down through the marrow of my jawbone. My poetics changed rapidly.

3. Brooks, "Lectures on Preaching" in *Theories of Preaching,* p. 16.
4. Sternberg, *The Poetics of Biblical Narrative,* p. 2.

Multisyllabic words turned to groans while the world in my head reduced itself to a single reality: the pain in my mouth. I experienced in a small way Elaine Scarry's observation that "Physical pain — is language destroying."[5]

The intensity of this small experience reveals in brighter light how our language is rooted in the physicality of our being. The character of my articulation changed as my historically conditioned imaginative construction of the world was reduced to the sensations in my jaw.

I had a prescription for codeine tablets to dull the pain, and within a day or two the character of my articulation of the world shifted from groans back to complete sentences. But all of us who have the advantage of being comfortable enough to speak need to recall that we live in a world where pain is constantly being used to destroy the poetics of others. Scarry records how torture not only "inflicts bodily pain that is itself language-destroying, but . . . also mimes (objectifies in the external environment) this language-destroying capacity in its interrogation, the purpose of which is not to elicit needed information but visibly to deconstruct the prisoner's voice."[6]

Scarry's observation about what happens to our ability to use language under torture diffuses any romanticized understanding of poetics. A thorough examination of our poetics will lead us to consider the conditions of privilege or oppression that are giving rise to the way we speak and write.

Our poetics is always a function of our historically conditioned imaginative construction of the world that we fashion from our physical existence in time and space. In a period of relative stability and prosperity, we may not be aware of the direct connection between our poetics and our life situation. Our poetics will tend to reinforce our privileged existence so that we value its conventions as part of the social structure that ensures our comfort. But let that life situation be disrupted, and we will scramble for a new poetics so that our speech more accurately expresses our world. Thus, for example, Czeslaw Milosz, winner of the 1980 Nobel prize in literature, reflects how the terrors of World War II stripped away the romantic conventions of literature that had hitherto been a part of the cultural currency of Poland:

5. Scarry, *The Body in Pain: The Making and Unmaking of the World* (New York: Oxford University Press, 1985), p. 19.
6. Scarry, *The Body in Pain*, pp. 19-20.

> A great simplification of everything occurs, and an individual asks
> himself why he took to heart matters that now seem to have no weight.
> And, evidently, people's attitude toward the language also changes. It
> recovers its simplest function and is again an instrument serving a
> purpose; no one doubts that the language must name reality, which
> exists objectively, massive, tangible, and terrifying in its concreteness.[7]

"The language must name reality" — that is a primary criterion for the
evaluation of all sermons, but we have no way of being sure we meet that
standard if we never examine our poetics of the pulpit. A simple appeal
to the language of Scripture and tradition is not sufficient, because such
an appeal assumes that the verbal strategies of faith and theology are
sufficiently self-explanatory in themselves, when in fact they are inevitably
mired in the understandings and values of those who employ the language
of belief. For example, resistance to inclusive language is often cloaked in
Biblespeak — the repetition of received language without an examination
of its internal poetics (the way it functions within Scripture and tradition)
or its applied poetics (the way it functions now).

The Redemption of Fallen Language

Examining our poetics makes us honest about our words, compels us to
see that preachers and believers are no less immersed in the artifice of
language than people of other systems of belief or disbelief. Recognizing
this is a necessary part of faithfulness: it saves us from making our words
idols, from forgetting that God is spirit, not language:

> Far easier to melt the gold
>   and smash the brittle clay
> Of idols that the hand may mold
>   Than change the way we pray.
> How tempting for the church to seize
>   Upon familiar forms,
> Retreating to antiquities
>   To hide from present storms.

7. Milosz, *The Witness of Poetry* (Cambridge: Harvard University Press, 1983),
p. 80.

As Judah vainly sought escape
    Behind the temple walls,
The sermons, hymns and prayers we shape
    May mute the God who calls.

Lord, give your church the grace to bend
    From its constricted pose
That we who bear your name may tend
    To where you Spirit blows.

The ancient forms may yet renew
    In us their first intent:
To bring and keep us close to you
    Through prayer and sacrament.[8]

The problem for the poet is the constriction of the imagination, the retreating to antiquities and hiding behind the temple walls, circumscribing the possibilities of the Spirit within the human definitions of the sacred. Our religious creations "may mute the God who calls." Yet the poem makes its case by employing the most common meter of English hymnody, utilizing traditional religious terms, and envisioning revitalization as the fulfillment of original intent. The verses demonstrate in compressed form the circularity of all poetics, even those that are prophetic or revolutionary: they employ a fallen language inherited from the past, with all its distortions and limitations.

> The language of the subject is also fallen. Like Adam, we are not separate from language, however distant from it we may be; we are inextricably involved with it, and are ourselves . . . a text, a tissue of words. In our case, however, since the constitution and also the well-being, the possibilities, of the subject depend, in ways and to an extent that we fail to understand, on the language in which it states itself and its connections with what it takes to be not itself, if language is fallen we fall with it. Language comes to us, from a past, from a social experience, that are evil; we are named, not by words that are ours, or that are unused, but by the words we inherit, and those words are entangled, obscure, tired.[9]

---

8. Thomas H. Troeger, "Far Easier to Melt the Gold," copyright © 1987.
9. Michael Edwards, *Towards a Christian Poetics* (Grand Rapids: William B. Eerdmans, 1984), pp. 130-31.

All one has to do is think of a great simple word that is common to the pulpit and to everyday speech to appreciate how "entangled, obscure, and tired" our words are. Take *love,* for example. Think of its commercial, exploitative uses on television. Think of its erosion through theological cliches from the pulpit and its trivialization on bumper stickers: "HONK IF YOU LOVE JESUS." Then recall when you have known the love of God, and compare the distance between the reality and the word and you will have some sense of how fallen our language is. The sharpness of that contrast becomes apparent when we attend to the poetics of the pulpit. Our goal is not simply to become more relevant or eloquent or engaging. We want to redeem language so that our words may more genuinely invite belief in the Word who redeems the world.

Traditional Christian Poetics

Homileticians and people in the related fields of liturgy and hymnody have been working on the poetics of Christian proclamation, without necessarily using the term, since the time of the New Testament writers. Paul the apostle makes clarity of understanding a guiding principle for the church at Corinth (1 Cor. 14), and that standard of judgment prevails in much of the most influential preaching literature today. Reading Richard Lischer's *Theories of Preaching,* an anthology of homiletical selections spanning the centuries, I was struck by how often the appeal was made for clear, direct language in the pulpit. Alan of Lille wrote that the sermon "is composed to instruct the souls of the listeners, so that they may concentrate, not on who is speaking to them, but on what he is saying." Charles G. Finney affirmed that "preaching, to be understood, should be colloquial in its style. A minister must preach just as he would talk. . . . This lofty, swelling style will do no good." John Broadus asserted that "in all speaking, especially in preaching, naturalness, genuineness, even though awkward, is really more effective for all the highest ends, than the most elegant artificiality."[10]

The poetics of directness and clarity have often been joined with a rhetoric of persuasion. There is, for example, a forensic overtone in

10. Alan of Lille, Finney, and Broadus, in *Theories of Preaching,* pp. 12, 118, and 233, respectively.

1 Peter when the author writes, "Always be prepared to make a defense to any one who calls you to account for the hope that is in you, yet do it with gentleness and reverence" (3:15b). Although the passage does not necessarily carry the connotation of being called before an official of the state, the word *defense (apologia)* was commonly used in the context of court proceedings.

Classical rhetoric heightened the forensic tone of homiletics, especially after Augustine wrote *De Doctrina Christiana,* which "made it possible for Christians to appreciate and teach eloquence without associating it with paganism."[11]

The poetics of directness and clarity achieves perhaps its purest expression in the Reformed tradition, in which worship is centered in the sermon and congregational hymnody. This is evident not only in tradition's approach to preaching but in its entire ethos of corporate prayer: "From the architecture, from church furnishings, from the congregational music, from the Geneva gown of the pastor himself, everything breathes *simplicity, sobriety,* and *measure* — which are precisely the qualities that Calvinist aesthetics demands of the art-object."[12] This is a poetics of "artistic *kenosis,*" an emptying out of all that is ornamental, as exemplified in the work of Isaac Watts, who "had to lay his poetic glories aside, and dress the profound message of the gospel in homespun verse and the language of the people."[13]

This artistic *kenosis* resulted in what Donald Davie has called "the plain style," in which images are used "sparingly" and seldom sought "except in commonplaces."[14] However, the plain style was in fact a self-consciously practiced form of poetics. Watts confessed the difficulty of trying to maintain such an approach: "It was hard to restrain my verse always within the bounds of my design."[15] Even simplicity is an artifice. Preaching straight from the Bible always involves preaching crooked from

11. George A. Kennedy, *Classical Rhetoric and Its Christian and Secular Tradition from Ancient to Modern Times* (Chapel Hill, N.C.: University of North Carolina Press, 1980), p. 159. For a summary and critical analysis of *De Doctrina Christiana,* see pp. 153-60.

12. Donald Davie, *A Gathered Church: The Literature of the English Dissenting Interest, 1700-1930* (New York: Oxford University Press, 1978), p. 25.

13. Harry Escott, quoted by Davie in *A Gathered Church,* p. 106.

14. Davie, *The New Oxford Book of Christian Verse* (Oxford: Oxford University Press, 1981), p. xxvi.

15. Watts, quoted by Davie in *A Gathered Church,* p. 106.

the Bible. We inevitably bend things to our idea of straight as informed by our historically conditioned imaginative construction of the world.

The Shift from Traditional Poetics

During the modern period our imaginative construction of the world has become more and more complex, leaving us less and less certain that the language we have inherited adequately expresses the reality we experience. Just as the general poetics of Western literature "is distinguished by a gradual dislocation of traditional standards based on the neoclassical interpretation of Aristotle's *Poetics* and on the models of classical antiquity,"[16] so there has been a proliferation of approaches to the shape and style of sermons, calling into question the grip of traditional rhetoric on homiletics. In part, this reflects the observation of Phillips Brooks already cited, that "preaching in every age follows, to a certain extent, the changes which come to all literature and life."

Peter S. Hawkins has made a study of how this shift has affected the work of three creative writers — Flannery O'Connor, Walker Percy, and Iris Murdoch — who have struggled mightily "to tell the story of transcendent experience in a period when people commonly lack the words to express it and therefore the means by which to enter it more deeply."[17] Hawkins calls their efforts "Strategies of Grace," a phrase that suggests the high self-consciousness about language that is part of post-modern theology. Like the writers whose work Hawkins analyzes, preachers need a verbal strategy, a theological poetics for the pulpit that takes into account how "the whole theological frame of reference, concretely expressed in Scripture, that once provided the coherence for Western culture and imagination . . . does so no longer."[18]

Hawkins's bold statement of our cultural situation helps to explain why homiletics in recent decades has paid so much attention to communications theory and the design of sermons. At their shallowest, such efforts become merely techniques, but at their best they represent an

16. *Princeton Encyclopedia of Poetry and Poetics,* ed. Alex Preminger (Princeton: Princeton University Press, 1974), p. 503.

17. Hawkins, *The Language of Grace* (Cambridge, Mass.: Cowley Publications, 1983), p. 4.

18. Hawkins, *The Language of Grace,* p. 1.

awareness of the need for "strategies of grace" to facilitate the reception of the gospel.

The difficulties that Hawkins traces in his study of O'Connor, Percy, and Murdoch are also evident in the turbulent state of biblical interpretation, theology, and hermeneutics. I am certain that there are more than two ways of looking at this situation, but two come immediately to mind. One is to assess the changes as a part of the chaos of our era, the breakdown of order, yet another attack on God and the integrity of God's Word. Although I never want to be so naive as to discredit the effects of sin on any human undertaking, including the emergence of a new homiletic, I believe another interpretation is more accurate: the post-modern shift in the poetics of theological expression represents nothing less than a revelation from God. I use the word *revelation* here in its primary meaning from the Greek, *apokalypto,* "to uncover." A new poetics is uncovering the truth about people, values, social structures, and experience that our inherited way of speaking had hidden.

I am not asserting that every shift of language is a revelation from God. We human beings say a lot of foolish things, especially in the name of God, and there is no need to believe that all changes in our patterns of articulation are holy and good. Jargon comes and goes, and a lot of it is a way of hiding rather than uncovering the truth of our existence. So when I refer to shifts in language being a revelation from God, I am thinking of those transformations that have a moral resonance, that are in harmony with the spirit of the gospel and hence provide "a witness that is life-giving for women and for men . . . a witness that enables us to make choices that are authentic and good, that are faithful to the deepest needs of the human community and consonant with its noblest aspirations."[19]

The revelation taking place through the shift in theological poetics is no sudden rending of the heavenly veil. It is more like a dawn that intermittently promises a day of clouds, then clear sky. For a while we see increasing brightness, then it clouds over again. But one thing we know for sure: the sun is coming up.

Because we are just beginning to glimpse what our new world will look like, our articulation of the reality is often tentative and awkward. For the time being, we live with an interim poetics of the pulpit, learning

19. Margaret A. Farley, "Feminist Consciousness and the Interpretation of Scripture," in *Feminist Interpretation of the Bible,* ed. Letty M. Russell (Philadelphia: Westminster Press, 1985), p. 41.

how to speak inclusively with the grace and assurance that belonged to the older poetics we are leaving behind. The word of God that will emerge through this process

> will never have the same monolithic uniformity for us that it has had for previous generations. We have become acutely aware of how insinuated that Word is in the crisscrossing complexity of the biblical words, of how interdependent that Word is on the conflict of images of God within Scripture. We have also become aware of our own situation-specific location in the structures of history, class, and gender.[20]

Charting the Shape of a New Poetics

Although a post-modern poetics for the pulpit will not be marked by "monolithic uniformity," certain characteristics of this new homiletic are already beginning to emerge and can help to guide us just as principles of classical rhetoric gave direction to our preaching ancestors. We need such an overview not in order to prescribe the future direction of homiletics but because, as M. H. Abrams notes in an essay on literary poetics,

> criticism without a theoretical understructure (whether this is developed explicitly or brought in merely as occasion demands) is made up largely of desultory impressions and of unassorted concepts which are supposedly given by "common sense," but are in fact a heritage from earlier critics, in whose writings they may have implicated a whole theoretical system.[21]

I recall a meeting of the Academy of Homiletics in which we experienced the confusion that results when there is an inadequate "theoretical understructure" for evaluating sermons. After having listened to a sermon presented in the classic rhetorical style, we had a conversation with the preacher about his sermon. The room divided into two sections. Those sitting up front near the preacher had been impressed with the clarity and persuasiveness of the outline, while those in the back were

20. Mark I. Wallace, "Theological Table-Talk: Theology without Revelation?" *Theology Today* 45 (July 1988): 213.
21. Abrams, in *Princeton Encyclopedia of Poetry and Poetics*, p. 648.

murmuring that it would have been a fine sermon for the 1950s but not
for the 1980s. Because the preacher was a guest, we were reluctant to
pursue the conflict over evaluative standards that was present in the room.
But I have not forgotten the scene. I have often seen it replayed as I have
listened to the comments of colleagues in responding to various sermons
in chapel or at services of ordination and installation.

    These experiences make clear that every judgment about a sermon
is laden with cultural values and theological presuppositions. But unless
we begin to identify a post-modern poetics for the pulpit with clarity, our
homiletical criticism will consist "of desultory impressions and of unas-
sorted concepts which are supposedly given by 'common sense.'"

Our Starting Point:
The Phenomenon of the Sermon as Received

The development of such a poetics begins not by defining first principles
or the essence of homiletics but by considering the actual phenomenon
of preaching as experienced by members of the congregation. This choice
of starting point is a part of what it means to be post-modern: no accepted
authority gains automatic acceptance. The authority we acknowledge is
the materiality of what happens unfiltered by the bias that things ought
to be this way or that way. Such a phenomenological perspective is reinforced by the belief that God does not need to be protected by our
presuppositions. To believe in God means we are free to be attentive to
what is. God will suffer no loss from our candid analysis of what is in fact
happening to members of a congregation during the delivery of a sermon.

    I speak of members of the congregation as opposed simply to
listeners because people process a sermon with all of themselves — not
just with their ears but with their eyes and bodies as well. If I am bored,
I process the sermon through my lower back and buttocks. If I am engaged
by the sermon, I am oblivious to the weakness in my back and the hardness
of the pew. One definition of homiletics might be "theology processed
through the body."

    The British novelist Barbara Pym has a fine scene in her early novel
Civil to Strangers in which she traces the way a sermon is being received
by the congregation. We do not hear more than a few brief sentences of
the sermon — probably about as much as many listeners hear! — but

through the author's omniscient eye we see the impact of those sentences on the congregation.

> The rector was pleased with the sermon he preached that Sunday. He had managed to work everything in rather well, and the central idea was most original. He began by talking about the Parable of the Talents, going on from there to the question, the challenge, almost, 'Do we make the most of our lives and opportunities.'
>
> 'Last week,' he said, 'I had tea with an old lady.'
>
> There was of course, nothing extraordinary in this. Rectors and vicars all over the country were having tea with old ladies every day. Especially, perhaps, in small country towns where old ladies are predominant.
>
> 'When I came upon her,' continued the rector, 'she was engaged in doing some very beautiful embroidery. Jacobean embroidery, I believe it is called, although I am not very well qualified to speak of such things,' he added deprecatingly, almost with a smile, or the nearest to a smile that was allowable in the pulpit.
>
> 'I remarked how beautiful her work was, how much more beautiful than any I had ever seen before.'[22]

These are the opening sentences of the chapter. Notice they describe the sermon from the preacher's perspective, and many of the classic homiletical issues are present. The outline is skillful: "He had managed to work everything in rather well." He has a text on which he has based his introduction: "He began by talking about the Parable of the Talents." He has named his theme: "Do we make the most of our lives and opportunities." He has found a choice illustration from experience that will evidently make sense to his congregation: "Rectors and vicars all over the country were having tea with old ladies every day." And his delivery is congruent with the established norms of pulpit decorum for this particular parish: he smiles "the nearest to a smile that was allowable in the pulpit."

But then the perspective shifts from the pulpit to the pew. Instead of hearing the preacher's words, we begin to see the impact on the consciousness of the congregation.

Who was this old lady? wondered some of the female members of the

---

22. Pym, *Civil to Strangers and Other Writings* (New York: E. P. Dutton, 1987), p. 90. Subsequent quotations from this work are taken from the pages that follow in the novel.

congregation, for they did embroidery, and the rector had not had tea with any of them last week. And yet whose work could be more beautiful than theirs? It was each one's private opinion that her work was much too good for the Parish Sale. One only did it because of the Good Cause and the dear rector.

The rector continues — " 'Some people don't put in enough stitches,' repeated the rector in a slow emphatic voice" — and Pym multiplies the number of perspectives on the sermon. There is Cassandra, a beautiful young woman married to a boring writer named Adam. In the course of the sermon, she comes to realize that she is "the old woman" the rector visited, and she is delighted with the preacher's ruse to hide her identity because it enables her to imagine life as a widow, freed at last from her husband. Meanwhile, Adam is sitting there annoyed with the preacher because he has quoted from Keats while ignoring Adam's own published work. Then there is Janie, the preacher's daughter, who is "whiling away the time by staring at Mr. Paladin," the curate, contemplating marriage to him. And finally there is the newcomer in town, Mr. Tilos, who is lusting for Cassandra and about whom there has been no small amount of gossip in recent weeks.

Pym's comic wit illumines the web of meanings, fantasies, and stories that holds the congregation together. What is the sermon? Is it merely the rector's words? Or is the sermon the motion of that web in response to the preacher? Or perhaps it is more accurate to speak of three sets of sermons:

1. The sermon the rector delivered.
2. The sermon as responded to by each individual.
3. The sermon that is defined as the conglomerate effect of all the individually heard sermons on the corporate life of the congregation.

At the very least, a post-modern poetics for the pulpit tends to the complexities of the sermon as a corporate event. It is a poetics that considers the total constellation of forces that are shaping the reception as well as the delivery of the sermon. It calls for a closer definition of the transaction between preacher and congregation and of the qualities of personal presentation that best serve to express and awaken the living truth of God in the congregation.

Personal Authenticity as the Expression
of Theological Credibility

Attention to the person or character of the preacher is not new. As Richard Lischer points out in the introduction of his anthology,

> Most homiletical treatises after Augustine and through the Middle Ages (e.g., Alan of Lille and Guibert of Nogent) deal with the authority, formation, and holiness of the one who is appointed to preach. The same concerns are evident in seventeenth, eighteenth, and nineteenth century classics on the ministry, whether by Baxter, Herbert, Spener, or Schleiermacher.[23]

A post-modern poetics of the pulpit seeks to clarify how that traditional concern for the character of the preacher is redefined by twentieth-century thought and experience. The rise of psychological culture since Freud and the atrocities perpetuated through the quasi-religious appeals of tyrants have reshaped the way we think about "authority, formation, and holiness." I find in myself a reluctance to employ these terms too quickly for fear of covering the sharp issues of personal integrity and group dynamics with a veneer of religiosity. Sounding religious becomes suspect when we consider the pietisms of the despotic. Recent experience with the electronic church and the scandals attached to preachers in the public eye have only served to reinforce this suspicion.

To distinguish the difference between how the character of preachers used to be judged and how it is judged now, let's compare two poems that describe pulpiteers who lack the requisite personal integrity for their calling. The first is by the eighteenth-century poet Timothy Dwight, and the second is by the contemporary British poet C. H. Sisson.

> Here stood Hypocrisy, in sober brown,
> His sabbath face all sorrow'd with a frown.
> A dismal tale he told of dismal times,
> And this sad world brimfull of saddest crimes;
> Furrowed his cheeks with tears for others' sin,
> But closed his eyelids on the hell within.
> There smiled the smooth Divine, unused to wound,
> The sinner's heart with hell's alarming sound.
> No terrors on his gentle tongue attend,

---

23. Lischer, *Theories of Preaching*, p. 3.

No grating truths the nicest ear offend.
That strange 'New Birth', that methodistic 'Grace'
Nor in his heart, nor sermons, found a place.
Plato's fine tales he clumsily retold,
Trite, fireside, moral see-saws, dull as old;
His Christ and Bible placed at good remove
Guilt hell-deserving, and forgiving love.
' 'Twas best,' he said, 'mankind should cease to sin;
Good fame required it; so did peace within.'[24]

Even before we consider the content, we are struck by the refinements of the style, the regularity of the meter, the use of rhymed couplets, and the patrician elegance that hones to a keen edge the blade of sarcasm.

The charge against this pulpiteer, however, is much less refined than the mannered poetics: "Here stood Hypocrisy. . . ." The poet draws his portrait from a perspective of absolute conviction about the doctrine of the gospel. There is a precise and clear standard of poetics for the pulpit: congruence between the one true theology and the speech and behavior of the preacher.

Although concern for theological integrity does not disappear when we turn to the poem by Sisson, it is expressed in a different fashion, reflecting the impact of post-Freudian psychological culture. The poet addresses his lines to John Donne, known not only for his poetry and preaching but also for the passionate loves of his youth:

You brought body and soul to this church
Walking there through the park alive with deer
But now what animal has climbed into your pulpit?
One whose pretension is that the fear
Of God has heated him into a spirit
An evaporated man no physical ill can hurt.

Well might you hesitate at the Latin gate
Seeing such apes denying the church of God:
I am grateful particularly that you were not a saint
But extravagant whether in bed or in your shroud.
You would understand that in the presence of folly
I am not sanctified but angry.

24. Dwight, "The Triumph of Infidelity," in *The New Oxford Book of Christian Verse*, p. 206.

> Come down and speak to the men of ability
> On the Sevenoaks platform and tell them
> That at your Saint Nicholas the faith
> Is not exclusive in the fools it chooses
> That the vain, the ambitious and the highly sexed
> Are the natural prey of the Incarnate Christ.[25]

Here the measure of homiletical credibility is not the correctness of dogma but the authenticity of the preacher's humanity. This shift in standards is not a matter of reducing theology to psychology, however. The point is that such authenticity stands in the service of making clear the gospel: "the vain, the ambitious and the highly sexed/Are the natural prey of the Incarnate Christ." Notice here the economy of traditional religious language. We do not expect the final two words; we might more naturally expect to read, "the vain, the ambitious, and the highly sexed/Are the natural prey of commercial exploitation." But Sisson suggests that they are the "natural prey of the Incarnate Christ." He ends the poem at the center of the gospel — the Incarnate Christ — and in that way renders it as theologically faithful as Timothy Dwight's.

But how different the poetics, the manner by which that point is achieved. Dwight sees hypocrisy in replacing the gospel and its severities with a life that pleasures in the flesh. Later point in the poem, Dwight describes how the preacher "Most daintily on pampered turkeys dined;/ Nor shrunk with fasting, nor with study pined." But Sisson sees hypocrisy in the denial of the flesh, in the inauthenticity of the preacher who thinks himself "An evaporated man no physical ill can hurt." A disembodied preacher cannot credibly proclaim the Incarnate Christ.

This yearning for someone in the pulpit who is fully in touch with her or his humanity represents the secularization of the holiness of the preacher. At its worst, such a poetics results in preachers sharing inappropriately about themselves and using the pulpit to meet their own needs instead of declaring the gospel. But this distortion of a poetics of authenticity does not invalidate what Sisson is getting at in his poem. For when such a poetics is exercised with faith and grace, preaching becomes nothing less than a medium of salvation.

Philip Hallie gives us a powerful example of this in his description of Pastor André Trocmé, who led his congregation into a heroic ministry

---

25. Sisson, "A Letter to John Donne," in *The New Oxford Book of Christian Verse,* p. 285.

of saving Jews from the Nazi Holocaust. André's brother Francis recorded the impact of one of the preacher's sermons during the occupation:

> He is a pulpit orator who is absolutely original, who surpasses in authority anyone I have ever heard speak from the *chaire*. He begins in a simple, familiar mood, starting with recent events, everyday or religious, then he raises himself, little by little, analyzes his own feeling and thought, confesses his own heart with a sincerity and a perspicacity which disturb one; he uses the popular language, and sometimes crude language. . . . Is he not going to fall into trivialities? But no! See him there raising himself up . . . he climbs, climbs always higher . . . he draws us to the peaks of religious thought . . . and once we are at the summit, he makes us hover in a true ecstasy; then gently . . . he descends slowly to earth and gathers you in a feeling of peace which gives the last word "Amen" all the meaning the word has etymologically. One sits there afterwards . . . eyes clouded with tears, as if one has been listening to music that has seized you by your entrails.[26]

No preacher can grab us by the entrails who is not in touch with his or her own fundamental humanity. That is why Sisson says in his poem, "Bring out your genitals and your theology." Unless we face the physicality of our being and its place in driving us to preach, we will have a tendency to become inauthentic, to preach as though the goal for our listeners is to attain the "evaporated" state of the parson in Sisson's poem.

A passion for defining what constitutes effective human authenticity in the pulpit illumines the homiletical studies of Hans van der Geest. Drawing on his analysis of two hundred worship services as well as interviews with parishioners, he arrives at the same principle that Sisson achieves through poetic inspiration:

> I will awaken deep experiences in others to the extent that I am able to reach myself. If I overplay feelings of revenge because they are indeed terrifying, or if I rationalize a pious faith in order to agree with a theological theory, then I am closing myself off, and in the worship service I am drawing from a well which is going dry. That level of yearning and security is reached only by preachers who also seek access to their own interior, an interior which at first glance normally appears comical, childish, and not really ready to be shown in public. Preachers

---

26. Philip Hallie, *Lest Innocent Blood Be Shed: The Story of the Village of Le Chambon and How Goodness Happened There* (New York: Harper & Row, 1979), p. 171.

with compulsive tendencies become so afraid that it's painful for them to find that path to themselves.[27]

This is not self-display but the use of the self to identify the deep common core we share with other human beings. Again and again in preaching class I have seen these understandings of the self confused. Frequently students use unresolved, intimate stories about themselves to help explicate the biblical text or doctrine or theological tradition at the heart of the sermon. Apart from the delivery of the personal story, the students' eyes often grow dull and their voices obsequious as they relate the truth that "ought to be believed." The congregations are typically embarrassed by the personal stories, and they begin to focus on how to care for the person in the pulpit. Interest in the text is derailed, since it has been presented as an authority that cannot be questioned or challenged anyway.

When we untangle the mixed responses of a congregation after such a sermon, we often discover that the preacher's strategy can be traced back to an unacknowledged resistance to the passage or doctrine supplying the theological warrant for the sermon. To use van der Geest's terms, such preachers are rationalizing "a pious faith in order to agree with a theological theory," and thus "closing" themselves off.

Amazing things begin to happen when we ask these preachers to tell about the process of creating the sermon. They tell how they struggled with the text, resisting and fighting it in their hearts even while they made dutiful notes and sketched an outline of the message. As the preachers speak the truth of what happened to them, other members of the class begin to acknowledge their own ambiguities, and life is illumined. Van der Geest believes this kind of honesty is essential to the creation of contemporary sermons: "Contact with oneself is of decisive importance while preparing a sermon. The idea for the sermon emerges only in a creative restlessness, when the preacher dares ignore those constricting thoughts acquired elsewhere, thoughts that will be needed again only when it is time to examine the ideas."[28]

Van der Geest is performing an invaluable service to homiletics by getting us to look at the exposed nerve of preaching, the sermon as it is actualized through the preacher and the response of the congregation. It

27. Van der Geest, "Presence in the Pulpit," in *Theories of Preaching,* p. 85.
28. Van der Geest, "Presence in the Pulpit," p. 85.

is from this ganglion of dynamics that the real theology of the sermon emerges.

Authenticity as Shaped by Gender and Culture

Yet theological education has often devalued and obscured the complexities that van der Geest identifies as central to how people respond to a preacher. "In formal training the word 'objective' is quickly equated with 'avoidance of existential areas.' Faith can quickly be reduced to theology, and thus life to a theory, and for young theologians this often means they lose contact with the roots of their vocational choice."[29] Now, however, that situation is changing. A poetics of personal authenticity for the pulpit is emerging in North America through the impact of women clergy and through an increasing sense of the pluralism of the world and the church. Faced with a greater spectrum of homiletical styles, we are coming to appreciate that many of our so-called objective standards are in fact the expression of our gender and the values and politics of the communities that have raised us.

I would not want to characterize any one style of preaching as exclusively male or female for fear of dishonoring individual gifts. Nevertheless, I believe that what scholars have discovered to be distinctive about women's writing is also distinctive about their preaching:

> The formulation that female identity is a process stresses the fluid and flexible aspects of women's primary identities. One reflection of this fluidity is that women's writing often does not conform to the generic prescriptions of the male canon. Recent scholars conclude that auto-biographies by women tend to be less linear, unified, and chronological than men's autobiographies. Because of the continual crossing of self and others, women's writing may blur the public and private and defy completion.[30]

Before we criticize such an approach in the pulpit on the basis of an ostensibly objective theology, we need to ask if the true source is not our

29. Van der Geest, "Presence in the Pulpit," p. 83.
30. Judith Kegan Gardiner, "On Female Identity," in *Writing and Sexual Difference,* ed. Elizabeth Abel (Chicago: University of Chicago Press, 1982), p. 185.

disappointment that the sermon "does not conform to the generic pre-
scriptions of the male canon."

Virginia Woolf claimed that "a woman's writing is always feminine;
it cannot help being feminine; at its best it is most feminine; the only
difficulty lies in defining what we mean by feminine."[31] I believe we are
facing the same situation in homiletics. The gathering witness of women
in the pulpit will disclose over time the shape of this new poetics. Meanwhile, women's preaching will in part be an expression of the continuing
search "to celebrate uniquely female powers of creativity without perpet-
uating destructive feminine socialization."[32]

Recognizing the Projective Nature of Our Poetics

Some readers may protest that preaching and the theology that feeds it
should not seek to celebrate either female or male powers of creativity,
that the task of the pulpit is to declare God's initiative toward us in creating
and redeeming the world. But a preacher's declaration of God's initiative
is no less a human formulation about the nature of the Divine than any
other. It still depends on human language and human creative skills in
employing that language.

The time has come for the church to face honestly the projective
nature of all human talk about God. Such an acknowledgment does
nothing to corrupt our belief in the One who braided the fibers of the
brain and filled it with electrochemical juice in such a manner that the
configuration of cells would give rise to a consciousness that seeks to know
and adore the source of creation. When I consider the complexities of the
physiological and environmental factors that can lead to such projective
speech, I find myself "lost in wonder, love, and praise."

There is, then, no need to hide from the projective nature of
religious language for fear we will lose our faith in God. Besides, that
strategy is no longer available to us. Third World and feminist theologies
have demonstrated that the inherited imagery for God and the under-

31. Woolf, quoted by Elaine Showalter in "Feminist Criticism in the Wilderness,"
in *Writing and Sexual Difference*, p. 14.
32. Susan Gubar, " 'The Blank Page' and Female Creativity," in *Writing and Sexual
Difference*, p. 92.

standings of humanity flowing from that imagery are biased by our experience and are in collusion with oppressive social structures. The effort to delineate an articulation of transcendence that is beyond critique keeps failing because on our multicultural globe people live in a plurality of imaginatively constructed worlds and so their expressions of reality differ in profound ways. Since the gospel is about compassion and justice for all people, the church has to find some way of proclaiming a redeeming vision for humanity without the absolutism of universal dogmatic assurance.

The great Japanese writer Shusaku Endo demonstrates how complex this is in his novel *Silence,* which records the efforts of some Christian missionaries to Japan during the 1600s, when the native rulers had decided to make the Christians retract their faith. Although the work can be read as a historical novel, the force of the language and the conflict of cultures suggests that the author is in fact exploring the meaning of religious language and truth for our own time. Father Rodrigues, the main character, is brought before a panel of samurai who question him:

> The samurai on the extreme right said in a voice charged with emotion: "Father, we are deeply moved by the strength of your determination in coming here from thousands of miles away through all kinds of hardships. Undoubtedly you have suffered deeply."
>
> There was a gentle tone in his words, and this very gentleness pierced the priest's heart, giving him pain.
>
> . . . "Father, we are not disputing about the right and wrong of your doctrine. In Spain and Portugal and such countries it may be true. The reason we have outlawed Christianity in Japan is that, after deep and earnest consideration, we find its teaching of no value for the Japan of today."
>
> The interpreter immediately came to the heart of the discussion. The old man in front with the big ears kept looking down on the priest sympathetically.
>
> "According to our way of thinking, truth is universal," said the priest, at last returning the smile of the old man. "A moment ago you officials expressed sympathy for the suffering I have passed through. One of you spoke words of warm consolation for my traveling thousands of miles of sea over such a long period to come to your country. If we did not believe that truth is universal, why should so many missionaries endure these hardships? It is precisely because truth is common to all countries and all times that we call it truth. If a true

doctrine were not true alike in Portugal and Japan, we could not call it 'true.'"

. . . The interpreter slowly translated the words of yet another samurai. "A tree which flourishes in one kind of soil may wither if the soil is changed. As for the tree of Christianity, in a foreign country its leaves may grow thick and the buds may be rich, while in Japan the leaves wither and no bud appears. Father, have you never thought of the difference in the soil, the difference in the water?"

. . . The priest lowering his eyes spoke quietly. "No matter what I say, you will not change your minds. And I also have no intention of altering my way of thinking."[33]

Notice that there is a moment of human connectedness in the midst of the confrontation. It comes at the point of identifying with human pain. The first samurai who speaks acknowledges how the priest has suffered, and that acknowledgment brings a moment of profound human understanding: "There was a gentle tone in his words, and this very gentleness pierced the priest's heart, giving him pain."

But a few paragraphs later the priest refers to that pain not in order to claim their common humanity but in order to win his argument: "If we did not believe that truth is universal, why should so many missionaries endure these hardships?" The actual universal truth — that people suffer and that the identification of our pain by another penetrates to the heart — this truth gets buried beneath the priest's urgent attempt to persuade the samurai of the truth of his case. His is a classical forensic appeal, making a claim to universal truth that can be persuasively argued.

A post-modern homiletics does not so quickly grab at the right verbal formulation. Instead, it begins at the level of human suffering and the trust and empathy awakened when our pain is recognized by another. Endo makes it clear that it was this quality, not the classical homiletics, that first won a hearing for the gospel in Japan. Ironically, Father Rodrigues understood this at an earlier point in his career. Here is his description and analysis of why the efforts of his missionary predecessors were effective:

I tell you the truth — for a long, long time these farmers have worked like horses and cattle; and like horses and cattle they have died. For the first time they have met men who treated them like human beings.

33. Endo, *Silence,* trans. William Johnston (New York: Taplinger, 1980), pp. 166ff.

It was the human kindness and charity of the fathers that touched their hearts.[34]

Notice the definition of truth here: the suffering of the people. The difference between this blood-and-sweat understanding of truth and the disembodied argument Rodrigues later has with the samurai about universal truth is the difference between a poetics that starts with the materiality of our existence and one that works from the assumption of a superior truth that is not smudged with experience.

Imagine what might have happened had Father Rodrigues not been so anxious to debate the nature of universal truth but had instead given some indication of what had happened to his heart when the samurai said he had suffered. Of course, it is only a novel, and even in real life, recognition of our common humanity through suffering is only the *beginning* of understanding. But it is the kind of beginning that continues in spirit the beginning of the gospel: Emmanuel, God with us, the identification with human suffering, a willingness to lay aside the prerogative of transcendence to be fully present with a world in pain.

Our preaching must be as humble as our God. We must be willing to restrain our religious language and the historically conditioned imaginative construction of the world that it represents so that our articulation of reality may be renewed by the source to whom we give witness. This may sound like blasphemy to those like myself who understandably cherish the language of faith with which we were raised. I am not talking about abandoning our inherited religious language but about purging and renewing it through disciplined and parsimonious use.

Throughout Endo's novel, Father Rodrigues keeps throwing against the sky his plea that God will speak and break heaven's silence in the face of the torturing of Christians. But it is only after Rodrigues himself has given up the public expression of his faith that Christ speaks to him: "I was not silent. I suffered beside you."[35] It is not necessary that preachers give up the public expression of their faith! But in a post-modern poetics of the pulpit, that expression will come out of the crucible of silence and suffering and out of an increasing openness to those expressions of truth that lie beyond the traditional articulation of our historically conditioned imaginative worlds.

34. Endo, *Silence,* p. 49.
35. Endo, *Silence,* p. 285.

Narrative and Imagery

Richard L. Eslinger

The End of an Age

The preaching-as-storytelling movement emerged right on schedule. With a certain inevitability, it blossomed within the past two decades in the context of the rise of the new post-critical biblical interpretation and the decline of the old rationalist and historicalist approaches to Scripture. On the one hand, a narrative homiletic was the consequence of antecedent explorations into narrative by literary critics and later by biblical scholars. With the usual cultural lag (about a decade in each case), the paradigm shift in interpretation produced its first fruits in homiletics.[1] On the other hand, the rapidity with which the storytelling homiletic gained popularity was due in no small part to the homiletical environment of the late 1960s and early 1970s. With the exception of a few prophetic voices, there was a homiletic vacuum of immense proportions.[2] Storytelling sermons offered signs of new life in the midst of the collapse of topical preaching.

Among the many factors contributing to the disarray in modern homiletics, none was more devastating than the paradigm shift in scriptural interpretation. If the historical model led to a dismantling of a text in

---

1. Charles Rice began exploring a storytelling homiletic in a series of articles. Then Rice, along with Edmund A. Steimle and Morris J. Niedenthal, produced the movement's Magna Carta, *Preaching the Story* (Philadelphia: Fortress Press, 1980).
2. One notable prophetic voice was that of David James Randolph in *The Renewal of Preaching* (Philadelphia: Fortress Press, 1969).

order to achieve a "world" behind its facade, preaching used the occasion to find the presumed "message" within that world. Such an approach was based on a hermeneutic of distillation, as David Buttrick notes: "This position assumes (1) that content can be separated from words, and (2) that content can be translated from our time-language to another without alteration, and (3) that such content can be grasped as an objective truth apart from particular datable words."[3]

It was in parable interpretation following Jülicher that this reductionist methodology was played out most clearly. The interpreter and the preacher both knew what to do when given a parable — locate its main idea and set aside the extraneous material. Parables were scenes out of daily life in first-century Palestine used by Jesus to illustrate some moral or religious point. That these "single points" of the same parable varied so much according to the theology and piety of the interpreter was only spotted much later by Norman Perrin.[4] It was Amos Wilder's genius to name the parable as a narrative metaphor,[5] a hermeneutic reframing that led Robert Funk to conclude, "Reduction of the meaning of the parables to a single idea . . . is only a restricted form of rationalization. . . . The metaphor must be left intact if it is to retain its interpretative powers."[6] The new criticism, as it was being incorporated within biblical scholarship, set itself against the whole reductionist tradition.

Foundations of a Narrative Theology

Decisive in this attack on the old criticism was Hans Frei's work *The Eclipse of Biblical Narrative*, published in 1974. Frei traced the eighteenth- and

3. Buttrick, *Homiletic: Moves and Structures* (Philadelphia: Fortress Press, 1987), p. 265.

4. See Perrin's *Jesus and the Language of the Kingdom* (Philadelphia: Fortress Press, 1976). He remarks that Jülicher's main ideas collection "looks very much like a manifesto of nineteenth-century theological literalism," whereas Jeremias's "looks very much like a summary of a rather conservative Lutheran piety" (pp. 105-6).

5. See Wilder, *The Language of the Gospel: Early Christian Rhetoric* (New York: Harper & Row, 1964).

6. Funk, *Language, Hermeneutic, and Word of God* (New York: Harper & Row, 1966), p. 136. For a survey of the recent history of parable interpretation and its homiletical implications, see my "Preaching the Parables and the Main Idea," *Perkins Journal* 37 (Fall 1983): 24-32.

nineteenth-century ideological roots of historicism, noting that "once literal and historical reading began to break apart, figural interpretation became discredited both as a literary device and as a historical argument."[7] Interpreters began to look for meaning outside or behind the stories themselves, either within the "real" history reported by the story or apart from history as mythic "truth." This bias within historical-critical interpretation led to a persistent confusion of "history-likeness" (the literal meaning of a narrative) and history itself. What followed, Frei argued, was "the hermeneutic reduction of the former to an aspect of the latter."[8] But in overlooking the significance of the "literal meaning" of a narrative (i.e., its realistic character), interpreters were overlooking the fact that genre is inseparable from meaning. "Meaning and narrative shape bear significantly on each other," Frei insisted, and the former cannot be sought external to the latter.[9]

While Frei was mounting his project to relocate meaning within the narrative, Stephen Crites was noting the narrative character of human experience itself. His catalytic work developed a psychology (in its classical expression as seen in Augustine) that could serve to integrate inner experience, the "mundane" stories of the world, and the sacred story. Crites argues that we will be able to integrate these three elements into a coherent whole only if we view the experience of human consciousness as being "in at least some rudimentary sense narrative."[10] While memory implicitly involves a sense of succession, it is still incomplete as a process of knowing. Only recollection can both render the data of memory into a significant ordering and convey the distinctive element of style. All knowing involves recollection, and the most direct and obvious means of recollecting is the telling of a story.[11] Moreover, all of the activity involving such knowing, including memory and anticipation, is embraced within the tension of present experience, a mode of consciousness that has a narrative form. "Narrative alone," says Crites, "can contain the full temporality of experience in a unity of form."[12]

7. Frei, *The Eclipse of Biblical Narrative* (New Haven: Yale University Press, 1974), p. 6.

8. Frei, *The Eclipse of Biblical Narrative*, p. 12.

9. Frei, *The Eclipse of Biblical Narrative*, p. 12.

10. Crites, "The Narrative Quality of Experience," *Journal of the American Academy of Religion* 39 (September 1971): 297.

11. Crites, "The Narrative Quality of Experience," p. 300.

12. Crites, "The Narrative Quality of Experience," p. 303.

In light of this analysis, it is not at all surprising that interpreters began to champion narrative as the predominant mode of expression in Scripture. Biblical narrative is incredibly rich in its literary expression, conveying the fullness of human experience in abundance. The ways in which this narrative intention is so richly achieved are at the heart of the efforts of Robert Alter, Edel Berlin, and others to explicate a poetics of biblical narrative.[13] Upon such foundations, moreover, others have argued the theological priority of story over the sort of "second order" discourse found in dogmatics and ethics as traditionally conceived.[14] Narrative is essential to a comprehension of the saving intent of Israel's God and, pointedly, the revelation of God in Christ. Without the story, the development of the theological task is, literally, unfounded. Narrative biblical texts, then, are neither ornamental nor disposable; they are never simply illustrative of certain divine "truths." What Michael Root affirms regarding the economy of redemption can be applied equally to all other aspects of Christian life and work:

> The Christian story and the life and the world of the reader do not exist in isolation, but constitute one world and one story. . . . The relation of story to reader becomes internal to the story. As a result, the relations between the story and the reader become storied relations, the sort of relations that are depicted in narrative. . . . These storied relations, rather than general truths the story illustrates, mediate between story and reader.[15]

Given this functioning of biblical narrative to mediate the relations between God, self, and world, a shift to a narrative homiletic is compelling. To preach by expounding "general truths" is to alienate oneself and the community of faith from the normative mode of the discourse of revelation — story.[16]

13. See Alter, *The Art of Biblical Narrative* (New York: Basic Books, 1981); Berlin, *Poetics and Interpretation of Biblical Narrative* (Sheffield: Almond Press, 1983); and *The Bible and the Narrative Tradition,* ed. Frank McConnell (New York: Oxford University Press, 1986).

14. See David Tracy, *The Analogical Imagination: Christian Theology and the Culture of Pluralism* (New York: Crossroad, 1986), pp. 408ff.

15. Root, "The Narrative Structure of Soteriology," *Modern Theology* 2 (January 1986): 147.

16. For an explication of the resultant preaching-as-story approach, see chaps. 1-3 of my book *A New Hearing: Living Options in Homiletic Method* (Nashville: Abingdon Press, 1987).

The Limits of Story

The emergence of story as a hermeneutic principle and homiletic method has not, however, met with universal acceptance. Even as the "storytelling" movement gained wide popularity, cautions and contention continued to follow in its wake. Of course, those who by virtue of training and ideological commitment remain convinced of the validity of a discursive homiletic tend to dismiss the preaching storytellers out of hand. But of more persuasive force are the critiques raised by those who are not beholden to the old homiletical orthodoxy but are themselves in some fashion or other also within the post-critical camp. The following objections are repeatedly raised by storytelling's fellow travelers:

1. *The biblical witness is not by any means all story!* Narrative is not the sole vehicle for expressing the divine Word. The literary critical scholars are the first to point out the diversity of literary genre within Scripture. Given the breadth of literary forms within the canon (poetry, proverbs, epistles, hymns, etc.), the adequacy of a story-based homiletic appears problematic.[17] Alter is careful to remind the reader that a considerable portion of what might be taken for narrative is really extended dialogue.[18] And his assertions concerning the Hebrew Scriptures obtain with respect to the New Testament as well. It would be less than accurate to characterize a Johannine discourse as a "story" as that term is conventionally understood, for example. Daniel Patte describes it as "a text with a mixture of narrative and argumentative features."[19] Beginning as dialogues, such discourses soon abandon the Johannine "rule of two" and trail off into monologues ambiguously attributed to Christ or the narrator. The key point here is that the "biblical story" is not all narrative.

2. *There are limits to the ability of story to express most profoundly the self and the human condition.* Due attention has not been paid, Richard Lischer contends, "to the ways in which story falsifies those vast and deep non-narrative domains of human life."[20] What lurks at the depth of the unconsciousness is not some sort of primordial narrative but fragments of

17. In this connection, Tom Long deals with five dominant literary genres in *Preaching and the Literary Forms of the Bible* (Philadelphia: Fortress Press, 1989). Two of the five relate to story: he devotes one chapter to narrative itself and one to parables.

18. See Alter, *The Art of Biblical Narrative*, pp. 63-87.

19. Patte, *Structural Exegesis for New Testament Critics* (Minneapolis: Fortress Press, 1990), p. 17.

20. Lischer, "The Limits of Story," *Interpretation* 38 (January 1989): 30.

dreams, distorted images, and anxiety. Therapeutic intervention is not a technique for getting to the root story of a dysfunction; rather, it overlays this storyless abyss with a "new kind of fiction."[21] Lischer also proposes limits to story imposed by abstraction and contraction, although his view that the latter (involving image and symbol) functions as an alternative to narrative may be questionable.[22] Particularly regarding the "limit" of contraction, involving as it does image, symbol, and metaphor, a more friendly notion of complementarity might be in order.

3. *Story may not provide an adequate hermeneutic for interpreting the biblical witness because of its inability to encompass the wholeness of revelation.* The issue here is not a matter of genre but of the dynamic of God's self-disclosure in Scripture. The Christian faith is intersected by vertical as well as horizontal axes, and David Buttrick concludes that "the reason why Christian faith cannot be contained within the category of 'story' is because, in addition to a horizontal God-with-us story line, there is a 'symbolic-reflective' aspect to Christian faith formed by the *character of Jesus Christ* and the nature of a 'being-saved' community."[23] Preaching does tell a story, but it also names a name — and that naming of the living symbol Jesus Christ both transforms the genre of the human story (gospel) and radically qualifies its plot.

Given these objections, the question emerges whether the issue is more the adequacy of narrative as a hermeneutic stance or the inadequacy of the preaching-as-storytellers to fully develop their hermeneutic foundations. The more extensive work of the narrative "fellow-travelers" would suggest that both issues obtain.

The Image and Narrative Theology

Within the field of ethics, a narrative-based movement has emerged to pose a serious challenge to the former ascendancy of liberalism's social ethics as well as the rules/situations methodological impasse.[24] Stanley

21. Lischer, "The Limits of Story," p. 30.
22. See my essay "Worlds That Shape Us," *Liturgy: Preaching the Word* 8 (Fall 1989): 53-57.
23. Buttrick, *Homiletic*, p. 14.
24. In this context, Stanley Hauerwas insists that "ethicists on both sides of the 'context versus principle' debate have made the same error: in focusing on 'the problem,'

Hauerwas, among a number of post-liberal ethicists, sees narrative as essential to the sustaining of Christian community. The distinctiveness of that community for ethics, he says, lies in the story-formed tradition that shapes it and that provides for virtues, both personal and communal, sufficient to enable moral agency. Narrative forms every community in spite of the claim of liberalism "that society can be organized without any narrative that is commonly held to be true."[25] It is critical for a Christian ethic to assess what sort of stories bind and shape a community, thereby determining its life. As a people of the biblical story, Christians are formed with virtues of truthfulness, hospitality, and peace — virtues distinctive to a community with a distinctive tradition. So, Hauerwas concludes, "The narrative of scripture not only 'renders a character' but renders a community capable of ordering its existence appropriate to such stories. Jews and Christians believe this narrative does nothing less than render the character of God and in so doing renders us to be the kind of people appropriate to that character."[26] To speak of ethical agency in a Christian sense, then, is to make central the issue of a community's character and to ask what virtues are necessary to sustain it in the midst of an alien world.

Within this context, it has become essential for these narrative ethicists to attend to the decisive role of imagery in human agency. Story by itself is not sufficient. Imagination is a necessary correlate to the function of story for ethical agency. Selves not only recollect and hope in a narrative-like process but also encounter images by which they come to understand themselves and their world. At root, the image "is simply a representation of the self or part of its world, either actual or possible, that has an immediacy and concreteness which conceptualizations lack."[27] Such representations correspondingly shape each person's imagination and thereby "determine what we can and do see, think, feel, and hence, how we act."[28] It is by facilitating self-recollection, and thus ethical agency, that images provide their distinctive hermeneutic function: they allow us to

---

both have tended to ignore the ethics of character" (*Vision and Virtue: Essays in Christian Ethical Reflection* [Notre Dame, Ind.: Fides Publications, 1974], p. 49).

25. Hauerwas, *A Community of Character: Toward a Constructive Social Ethic* (Notre Dame, Ind.: University of Notre Dame Press, 1981), p. 12.

26. Hauerwas, *A Community of Character*, p. 67.

27. David Bailey Harned, *Images for Self-Recognition: The Christian as Player, Sufferer and Vandal* (New York: Seabury Press, 1977), p. 2.

28. Craig R. Dykstra, *Vision and Character: A Christian Educator's Alternative to Kohlberg* (New York: Paulist Press, 1981), p. 77.

"see" a world. As David Harned notes, "We are free to act in some purposive fashion only within the world that we can see."[29]

This "visional ethic," as opposed to both situationist and legalist approaches, views ethical agency as a function of character and its virtues, which are inevitably formed by our stories and the images by which we envision self and world. Since this interplay of story and image is inherent in the human condition, it is critical that we be attentive to both if we wish to transform our moral life. Stories locate us within a community, shaping us for better or worse as persons of virtue, but images are also decisive for social and personal transformation: there can be no revelation unless the imagination is converted.[30]

> Revelation is the conversion of the imagination and takes place when the revelatory images become engrained in the psyche and provide the framework for our seeing and our living. . . . Adequate images are images that help us see more deeply and clearly into the world; they do not hide it from us or distort it.[31]

Whatever else is involved in such conversion, the transformation of one's imagination is decisive. It is the testimony of Christian faith that the images for the conversion of the imagination are revealed within Scripture and its story.

A Hermeneutic of Imagery

If one cannot do narrative theology without attending to the imagination, then a more extensive exploration of the house of the image is demanded. We will need to balance a theology of story with a theology of image, holding the two in tension. Fortunately, the etiology of imagery is being explored within several seemingly disparate fields of inquiry, and the "what," "how," and "why" of imagery is becoming clearer.

As a scholar of historical Christianity, Margaret Miles has found it necessary to balance attention to historical texts with attention to the images that accompany them and provide their visual environment. Those

29. Harned, *Faith and Virtue* (Philadelphia: Pilgrim Press, 1973), p. 26.
30. See Dykstra, *Vision and Character,* p. 78.
31. Dykstra, *Vision and Character,* pp. 79-80.

who address only the textual evidence leave history in the hands of language users and language shapers — who, says Miles, are almost exclusively male. A hermeneutic of images, on the other hand, opens the range of historical inquiry to women as well as men and offers "formulation and expression simultaneously to a wide variety of persons with different perspectives."[32]

Miles maintains that a hermeneutic of images is possible because texts and images share a susceptibility to many of the same canons of interpretation. Both yield their meaning only within some specific context (in each case genre is important), and both range from the more concrete and denotative to the more tensive and evocative. Miles grants that images tend to fall more toward the nondenotive end of the spectrum, although she locates the religious icon well toward the denotive pole (p. 34). She also asserts that the interpreter of imagery, "like the interpreter of texts, must determine the denotation of the image as a preliminary step to suggesting the spectrum of meanings it was likely to have had. [Images offer] a 'floating chain of signified,' a wide but finite range of possible meanings" (p. 35).

The commonality of texts and images, then, lies within their essentially historical character. Neither can be grasped out of context, nor can the meaning of either be isolated from a linguistic and cultural situation. Miles admits that texts do seem more susceptible to abstraction (though she argues that this is not always the case), but she maintains that the universality of images is grounded not in any such "detachable conclusions" but in "the capacity of the viewer to grasp in the concrete particularity of the image a universal affectivity" (p. 30). In fact, this capacity of imagery to achieve universality helps to show how images function individually. It is the capability of an image to generate and transform the affect, to move and focus the senses as well as the mind, that generates its power. Moreover, this power is inherently social and communal. Any given image will be interpreted "according to the viewer's interest, as informed by her or his physical experience, status within the community, education, and spirituality" (p. 34). Within the act of interpretation, the affections are both formed and transformed.

Visual images differ from texts in the extent to which they challenge

---

32. Miles, *Image as Insight: Visual Understanding in Western Christianity and Secular Culture* (Boston: Beacon Press, 1985), pp. 37-38. Subsequent references to this volume will be made parenthetically in the text.

the interpreter with their inherently multivalent character. Presentational rather than discursive, images naturally offer a variety of meanings, depending on the perspective from which they are viewed. In fact, this variety is inexhaustible; according to Miles, "the multivalence of an image means that we can never definitively interpret it" (p. 32). The codifiers of texts would be quick to characterize this as a limitation, but it could also be argued that this is precisely the genius of the image within human experience: it is radically available to all within the community, and it can convey transcendence and mystery in ways texts simply cannot. It is particularly the appeal of the image to the physicality of a person that differentiates it from a text. Our engagement with texts may evoke what has been called the "subjective consciousness," though only, says Miles, if we are equipped with "a comparatively high degree of linguistic training and skill, a level inaccessible to all but a few historical and contemporary people" (p. 36). Images, on the other hand, speak to and from physical existence, its range and its universality. "Visual images . . . are primarily addressed to comprehending physical existence, the great, lonely, yet universal preverbal experiences of birth, growth, maturation, pain, illness, ecstasy, weakness, age, sex, death" (p. 36). In short, images speak to life in the body.

Story and Image in Polarity

Logos and *icon* *should* be able to interact in faith and proclamation, but our actual experience has been that the two ways to knowing seem to yield increasingly dissimilar insights. Given to two paths, the Christian community perennially seems capable of focusing only on one or the other. At least three sets of polarities have produced obstacles to an integration of narrative and imagery within a single hermeneutic field.

1. The very emphasis on the mobility and "lifelikeness" of story stands in contrast with the static image as it presents itself in consciousness. This suggests an odd twist on Eugene L. Lowry's assertion in *Doing Time in the Pulpit:* the polarity here is not between conceptual "space" and narrative "time" but between *iconic* space and narrative time.[33] The issue

33. See Lowry, *Doing Time in the Pulpit: The Relationship between Narrative and Preaching* (Nashville: Abingdon Press, 1985).

was initially defined by Lessing in his *Laocoon* as a distinction between poetry and painting: poetry is "an art of time, motion, and action; painting an art of space, stasis, and arrested action."[34]

2. Miles has presented interpreters with a "text = cognition, image = affection" dichotomy. To the extent that this polarity is sustained, a unitive hermeneutics of narrative and imagery would seem to remain beyond our grasp.

3. A simplistic phenomenology also seems to offer a barrier to the achievement of some sort of intersection. Narratives are spoken and heard; images are portrayed and seen. Thus, even the human senses seem to conspire against an interaction of narrative and imagery.

All three of these ostensible dichotomies merit further consideration.

The Dynamic/Static Impasse

As Stephen Crites has noted, it is the sequential, time-conditioned movement of narrative that generates its unique "quality of human experience." Our experience is akin to that of story. We long to recollect our origins beyond the mere sequential listing of incidents that memory affords. And we strain to find intimations in present experience of some sort of ending, of denouement and fulfillment for our lives. Simply put, we seek to know God.[35] Perhaps our hunger for such narrative resolution is a legacy of exile from Eden;[36] at any rate, the experience of both temporary involvement and duration appears to be given within the world of narrative. On the other hand, the static, relatively unchanging character of the image also seems to be a given in our experience. The significance of an image is accessible and relatively defined within a single engagement. It yields a fullness of meaning in one take, in contrast to narrative, which yields its meaning only sequentially, over time (the reader at any given time is in

34. See W. J. T. Mitchell, *Iconology: Image, Text, Ideology* (Chicago: University of Chicago Press, 1986), p. 48.

35. "To know God," writes John Navone, "is compared to knowing the overarching or universal story, that is, to participate in it" (*Towards a Theology of Story* [Slough, England: St. Paul Publications, 1977], p. 41).

36. See Michael Edwards, "Story: Towards a Christian Theory of Narrative," in *Images of Belief in Literature,* ed. David Jasper (London: Macmillan, 1984). Edwards suggests that "we cannot imagine stories in Eden" (p. 179).

contact with only one point in the plot, not the whole). Herein lies the polarity: mobile stories and static images.

When preachers/interpreters confront this polarity of temporally based story and spatially based image, they typically adopt a series of Enlightenment assumptions. Even aside from the recent debates concerning the validity of this Enlightenment dogma within contemporary aesthetics, it seems safe to say that the dynamic-static contrast has traditionally been overdrawn. This is not to say that the contrast is wholly without merit, but it does seem to suggest that we can qualify our appropriation of it with social, linguistic, and ideological considerations. In other words, our hermeneutic will qualify the extent to which we view story as an exclusively temporal genre and image as an exclusively spatial genre.

There are already signs of an increasing interest in the spatial referents of the narrative performance of stories. Recent Markan scholarship, for example, has identified a spatial component of the Gospel that conveys theological as well as literary significance.[37] The Sea of Galilee functions in Mark as a boundary space between Jew and Gentile. The three crossings of this boundary by Jesus serve to announce the dissolution of an ethnic-based covenant in favor of a new Israel. But the context of the discussion still has to be expanded to encompass all narrative. W. J. T. Mitchell argues that spatial form "is no casual metaphor but an essential feature of the interpretation and experience of literature."[38] Most recently, Stephen Crites has explored the dimensions of spatiality in narrative, arguing that stories "create an intricate temporality and a no less intricate narrative space."[39] Although Crites speaks of "four spatial dimensions . . . as conditions of narrative truthtelling" (p. 114), in explicating them he actually locates five: social space, inner space, the celestial canopy, the supercelestial sublime, and the earthly ground.

1. *Social Space.* Crites defines social space as the "middle region of narrative space that supports all the other dimensions" (p. 101). Traditional cultures feature some *axis mundi* about which the society is organized, but modernity has either lost its centering sacred space or trans-

37. See, e.g., Werner H. Kelber, *The Kingdom in Mark: A New Place and a New Time* (Philadelphia: Fortress Press, 1974), pp. 48ff.

38. Mitchell, "Spatial Form in Literature," in *The Language of Images,* ed. W. T. J. Mitchell (Chicago: University of Chicago Press, 1980), p. 278.

39. Crites, "The Spatial Dimensions of Narrative Truth-Telling," in *Scriptural Authority and Narrative Interpretation,* ed. Garrett Green (Philadelphia: Fortress Press, 1987), p. 99. Subsequent references to this essay will be made parenthetically in the text.

formed that center into urban towers the force of which "is centrifugal rather than centripetal" (p. 104). Storytellers today need not be bound by the constraints of the shift from traditional social space with its sacred center to uncentered modernity, however. We should simply be listening for and telling stories that reconfigure our social space in imaginative and surprising ways.

2. *Inner Space.* Not specifically listed by Crites, inner space interacts with all other narrative space and has the capacity to reflect an exterior spatial dimension more precisely, to achieve a homology with it. So, for example, the inner space of a character in *Our Town* emerges as homologous with the sacred space of the village. On the other hand, the inner space of the characters in *Waiting for Godot,* in which the only *axis mundi* is a small barren tree in the second act, reflects a social space of desolation.

3. *The Celestial Canopy of Gods and Angels.* Hovering above our social space is a transcendent social space populated by the characters of the religious imagination. Beyond the typical tribal gods, says Crites, "are the high gods, the high goddesses, or the high God or Goddess" (p. 106). Angels may or may not resemble the beings of social space, but they are homologous with our inner space, "where thoughts and images fly free and stories pass among us" (p. 106). Given this "consonance between our inner space and the angelic transparency" (pp. 106-7), Crites offers a caution to those who would label the latter an imaginative projection of our inner habitations:

> To imagine is a spiritual act, a transportation of metaphors, nor is it impossible to suppose that the imagination itself is a spiritual medium formed in us by the bright spirits to provide the tabernaculum for their appearance, indeed to suppose that the inner space in which the imagination moves in such angelic fashion is hollowed out by the spirit in consonance with the heavenly ether in which the angels dwell. (P. 127)

4. *The Supercelestial Sublime.* It is our curse and blessing as moderns to know of a sublime emptiness that challenges all of our stories with its silence and its void. This "empty sublimity" has also moved deep within us, homologous with the boundless beyond. "The spirit that cries out of the depths, *de profundis,* to the height of heaven, now recognizes that this height and depth are the same, the boundlessness of outer space and inner space alike" (p. 110). Crites adds that the antidote for such an experience

of pathos is a quick return to our stories, whether sacred or profane. "Still, for us who bear this cold acosmic emptiness like a nitrogen bubble in our inner space, there can be no truth in a story that is not edged by this chill" (p. 111).

5. *The Earthly Ground.* In solidarity with Margaret Miles, Crites adds the special dimension of our earthiness, the "humus" of human being. We are "entirely of earth and earthly . . . digestive tracts, bags of water, hot air balloons, bundles of libidinous energy through which we are tricked into propagating our species" (p. 111). At every point we are linked to and with the earth. And although this dimension usually remains lurking in the narrative background, it is always there and inescapably so.

Having expanded on Mitchell's insights into the spatial aspect of narrative by pointing to these five dimensions, Crites has done much to lower the traditional barrier between story and image for those seeking to construct a new hermeneutic.

On the other side, the standing view of the image as something temporally static is also changing. We tend to think of the image in terms of a fixed visual reference, but in many cases an image may offer many different references. Imagine a large glass sculpture, for instance. The artifact itself remains passive, and yet the artist will have created it in such a way as to encourage you to move around it, adopting different points of view. Now, imagine that a second viewer enters the scene and accidentally bumps the sculpture, sending it crashing to the floor. Instantly, and tragically, you will have been exposed to a different kind of mobility in the image. Between two static experiences of the sculpture (one whole on the stand and the other in shards on the floor) an image-in-movement is etched into your consciousness. The significance of the image has expanded to include both these static and dynamic dimensions.

Given the spatial dimensions of narrative and certain aspects of mobility in our experience of images, it is clearly inappropriate to maintain that narrative is exclusively temporal and imagery exclusively spatial. In fact, I would argue that the traditional polarity is sufficiently diminished that it no longer constitutes a methodological barrier.

The Cognition/Affection Impasse

The second ostensible barrier between story and image involves the different ways in which we are said to negotiate them. Modern interpretation has tended to regard our encounters with texts as primarily a matter of cognition and our encounters with imagery as primarily a matter of focusing and generating affective responses. Moreover, if this difference in approach is as gender-specific as Miles suggests, the barrier between story and image is simply raised that much further. Can a world of rationalist, text-oriented males ever be reconciled with a world of affective, image-oriented females? Ironically, this quandary presents a striking resemblance to the old topical preaching cognition-affective polarization. In that case, the traditional multi-point sermon was held to be rationalist and propositional in character and hence lifeless, in need of some invigorating anecdotal material. As Charles Rice noted, that prescription never manages to produce anything like real life; the "projective-discursive style" only managed to produce "personality without personhood."[40]

In a careful assessment and reconstruction of aesthetic theory informed by Christian faith, Ella Bozarth-Campbell has attempted to create an incarnational poetics. Her basic strategy is to overcome the cognition-affection split by focusing on the enfleshed word. She notes that *logos* signifies the substance of the text as well as the activity of its utterance. As the word comes to life through the activity of speech, bodily presence is joined with that which is spoken.

> The interpreter becomes the incarnation of the poem by bringing her or his energy to it and by joining the two life forms in a presentational act. The word as life and light reverberates in the interpreter. . . . The interpreter becomes the sounding and visual presence of the literature, an icon, a being filled with sensuous form and structure, an iconic being that is *showing*.[41]

There is an erotic element in authentic interpretation that fuses *logos* and icon into one revelation. When this happens, cognitive and affective aspects of the word-event similarly coalesce. From the perspective of this incarnational poetics, Bozarth-Campbell reiterates the conclusion of two colleagues: "Antitheses of mind and body, thought and action are disastrous."[42] The unitive expression of word and image in performance

40. Rice, "The Expressive Style in Preaching," *Princeton Seminary Review* 64 (March 1971): 39.

41. Bozarth-Campbell, *The Word's Body: An Incarnational Aesthetic of Interpretation* (University, Ala.: University of Alabama Press, 1979), p. 55.

42. Wallace A. Bacon and Robert S. Breen, *Literature as Experience* (New York: McGraw-Hill, 1959), cited by Bozarth-Campbell in *The Word's Body*, p. 62. She also

reveals that body and mind, interpreter and text, cognition and affection all cease to remain discrete and separable entities. The word has become flesh.

The implications of all this for proclamation and liturgy are fresh and exciting. What if the preacher becomes an icon of the Word? In an act fully embodied, the one proclaiming the *logos* will be transformed by it. Within such an incarnational activity, language need not bifurcate into undue objectivity or subjectivity. With the immediacy designated by Buttrick as a "speaking of" rather than "talking about," the servant of the Word could become the bodily presence of the Word as well. The purpose of a text launched into the midst of a hearing community would serve to shape various aspects of the affective experience on the one hand, and imagery would help to provide a blend of cognitive insight and feeling, tone, and mood on the other.[43]

The Aural/Visual Impasse

A third ostensible barrier between word and image is so fundamental as to be virtually axiomatic. Texts, stories, and language all function within an oral/aural realm that has its own distinctive "grammar" of presentation. Images, too, operate with their own distinctive grammar of presentation involving a distinctly visual realm. These two realms have evolved different fields of inquiry and traditions of evaluation (going back at least as far as Plato and Aristotle). Within the biblical witness, *dabar/logos* clearly holds the dominant position in the territorial struggle between word and image. In the beginning was *logos,* and much of Scripture is the story of the consequences of the utterance of that divine Word. And yet the image maintains an essential presence as well: humanity is created by the Word as *imago Dei,* and in the incarnation of the Word we *see* the glory of the Father. Unfortunately, as Christian tradition has attempted to live out this biblical dialectic of Word and image, the two poles have often become

---

characterizes the dichotomy of gender-delineated modes of interpretation as disastrous. In response to Sontag's male/female hermeneutical alternatives, Bozarth-Campbell says, "I believe there are no 'masculine' nor 'feminine' qualities that cut irrevocably between the two sexes, that permanently exist in dichotomy, and that can define us simplistically along the narrow limits of gender. We are all the intricate sum of all that has gone before us and of the accidents of our cultural experience" (pp. 33-34).

43. On style, emotion, and point of view, see Buttrick, *Homiletic,* pp. 201-21.

rallying points for rival ideologies. Margaret Miles has offered some incisive instruction about the significance of imagery in early Christianity, noting that the early theologians remained remarkably inclusive on this point even while trinitarian and christological debates were hardening their language into credal forms.[44] It was not until much later that a split between the two was expressed first, in an iconoclastic revolt on behalf of the Word and then in the Protestant Reformation.[45]

Finally, the aural and visual worlds have become metaphors for different ways of understanding human identity. Visual experience keeps the world at a distance, objectifying it and allowing us to select what will be seen. Aural experience, on the other hand, is nonselective: we hear whatever sounds present themselves to us. Moreover, hearing invites an intimacy with things, inviting us to go inside them and ourselves.[46]

> In a visual cosmos, the self is an agent; in an aural world, it is a patient. In the former, the individual is safe, at least for the moment; in the latter, the individual is always vulnerable. In one world, the self is free; in the other, it is claimed, called to account, and asked to respond to the initiatives of others. In one realm the self is distinguished sharply from its environment; in the other, sounds bind it tightly to its social context and remind it of its contingency. One world contains only surfaces; in the other there are many and various clues to the interiority of selves.[47]

On one level, the kind of case being made by Harned and others regarding the distinctions between aural and visual worlds seems quite valid. There is a dialectic here that encompasses human experience and qualifies God's self-revelation as well. Nevertheless, Harned also reminds us that "the self is more than an organism."[48] We do well to heed the call of the narrative ethicists to engage in a thoroughgoing scrutiny of the

44. Miles, *Image as Insight*, pp. 55ff.

45. For a discussion of this iconoclastic tendency in the modern era, see Mitchell, *Iconology*, pp. 160-208. Concerning the iconoclastic impulse of the Reformation, Harned cites Martin Luther: "Even if you do not see you shall see by hearing. . . . He who will not take hold with his ears but wants to look with his eyes is lost. . . . Stick your eyes in your ears" (*Images for Self-Recognition*, p. 31).

46. See Walter Ong, *The Presence of the Word* (New Haven: Yale University Press, 1967), p. 6.

47. Harned, *Images for Self-Recognition*, p. 29.

48. Harned, *Images for Self-Recognition*, p. 23.

images through which we choose to view the world. But we also do well
to remember that our agency extends to the issue of which stories we
choose to form ourselves and our community. We have to take account
of the fact that we often mis-see what we look at and mis-hear what the
world presents to our ears. Some of these misperceptions are incidental
(e.g., Polonius's clouds in *Macbeth*), some are willful (e.g., the prophetic
indictment of Isa. 6:9-10),[49] and some are patently tragic (e.g., the com-
forting night sounds in Shusako Endo's *Silence*).[50] Still, no matter how
qualified it may be, there remains a dialectic between the oral/aural world
of story and the visual realm of imagery.

Word and Image in Convergence

That we should notice further signs of convergence, then, comes as a
surprise. But deeper explorations do, in fact, offer such signs. Bozarth-
Campbell continues to serve as our hermeneutic path-finder through her
analysis of the interplay of word and image in poetic performance. "*Logos*
as discourse," she says, "also means to reveal what one is talking about in
one's speaking." Then she adds, "The function of the *Logos* (Word) is to
let something be seen (image)."[51] By extension, the intent of narrative is
also "to let something be seen." We not only *see* the textures of character,
tone, and setting within the story but we experience self-revelation when
we engage them. At a more subjective level, the self is imaged in relation
to the story, while in a more public and liturgical context, the book is
raised as a monstrance with the words "This is the Word of the Lord."
Inevitably, it would seem, the intention of narrative and poetics is to reveal,
to bring the word to view.[52]

49. Isaiah repeatedly employs the images of seeing and hearing in diagnosing
Israel's disobedience and distress. Drunkenness is condemned precisely because it dulls the
senses to righteousness — with the result that the prophets of God's Word "reel with strong
drink" and hence "err in vision" (28:7). The Word of God to Isaiah, though, promises a
time of restoration when "the eyes of the blind shall be opened, and the ears of the deaf
unstopped" (35:5).

50. Endo, *Silence* (New York: Taplinger Press, 1976).

51. Bozarth-Campbell, *The Word's Body*, p. 39.

52. "Oral speaking connects word and image," says Bozarth-Campbell, "in that
it lets something be seen, shows something in an active sense" (*The Word's Body*, p. 106).

Approaching from the side of imagery, we may spot a similar dynamic at work — the tendency toward verbal expression, toward *logos*. In spite of popular assumptions, Mitchell says, images are not stable, static, or permanent in any metaphysical sense; in fact, they are not even "exclusively visual in any important way, but involve multisensory apprehension and interpretation."[53] Visual images "are inevitably conventional and contaminated by language."[54] And, Margaret Miles would add, they are susceptible to certain canons of interpretation in common with texts.[55] The case can also be made that some images are verbal and linguistic in character and not primarily visual at all: Mitchell includes linguistic images in his schematic of image along with the graphic, optical, perceptual, and mental.[56] Although the point remains somewhat controversial, literary critics and philosophers of language such as Paul Ricoeur argue that metaphor is the prime candidate for such categorization. Likening a metaphor to a verbal icon, Ricoeur speaks of the fusion of sense (meaning) and the sensible (perceptible to the senses) within the meaning of metaphor. Metaphor emerges in the imagination when "the figurative meaning emerges in the interplay of identity and difference . . . because the identity and the difference do not melt together but confront each other."[57] Speaking of the iconic function of metaphor, Ricoeur provides a place of intersection for Miles and Bozarth-Campbell:

> If metaphor adds nothing to the description of the world, at least it adds to the ways in which we perceive; and this is the poetic function of metaphor. . . . In its poetic function, therefore, metaphor extends the power of double meaning from the cognitive realm to the affective.[58]

Let us consider, then, the metaphor as a verbal image.

We have identified instances of fusion between word and image in iconic and metaphoric expression, but it remains the case that the two have not collapsed together. What we have, then, is a dialectic of word

---

53. Mitchell, *Iconology*, pp. 13-14.
54. Mitchell, *Iconology*, p. 42.
55. Miles, *Image as Insight*, p. 29.
56. See Mitchell, *Iconology*, p. 10.
57. Ricoeur, *The Rule of Metaphor: Multidisciplinary Studies of the Creation of Meaning in Language*, trans. Robert Czerny (Toronto: University of Toronto Press, 1977), p. 199.
58. Ricoeur, *The Rule of Metaphor*, p. 190.

and image, which may itself serve as a metaphor for interpretation. Perhaps the household of faith lives not beneath the historical-critical image of the hermeneutic "arch" but rather within an ellipse defined by two poles — Logos and icon, the Word made flesh that we have seen, and, having seen, have believed.

Intersections: Story and Imagery

Having argued for a hermeneutic inclusive of both word and image, I must now detail the interaction of images within one distinctive literary genre — narrative. I have been seeking to test the assumption of the visional ethicists that story and image are both theoretically compatible and functionally useful if held in tension. Now, with proclamation as the primary concern, the question becomes the "how" of this interplay of narrative and imagery. Not surprisingly, I will need to turn back to the narrative ethicists rather than the narrative homileticians for some insights in this regard.

First, we should note that stories — and biblical stories in particular — come ladened with images that potentially come to achieve a life of their own. (To further allegorize the Parable of the Sower, if the sower is the *story,* the seeds are *images.*) David Harned observes that images are found to inhabit narratives; without such habitation they become ambiguous. Since images are open to a variety of interpretations, it is the important role of the story to assign one (or some) from among them all. This "naming" of images, as we have noted, is the beginning step of moral agency. So, for example, there will be one set of consequences if the image of the self as sufferer is located within the myth of Sisyphus and quite another if it is located in the story of the cross. In one habitation, guilt is eternally unforgivable; in the other, the self can know forgiveness as well as an end to self-deception.[59]

If we cross-check narratives with an eye to this sort of imagistic function, we discover that the image may offer a perspective from which to view the story. Images offer a kind of lens through which we can read story — a kind of Bultmannian *vorverständnis.* So, for example, a person with a self-image of perennial guilt may be reading scripts of crises into

59. See Harned, *Images for Self-Recognition,* pp. 129ff.

the stories of congregational life. Images serve as hermeneutic lenses for stories, for better or for worse. Therefore, "images afford a critical perspective upon particular renditions of a story; the story provides critical perspective upon different interpretations of the imagery."[60]

Given this interplay between story and imagery, Gail Ramshaw's observation that images within Scripture exhibit a "Yes, No, Yes" kind of dynamic makes good sense.[61] "God is a rock," affirms the psalm, offering a verbal image in harmony with a covenantal/monarchical story. "God is *not* a rock," laments Israel when it tells the story of its exile. "God *is* a rock," sings the New Testament community as it recalls the Easter victory story of Christ its cornerstone. Images also have a way of undergoing metamorphoses within the communal consciousness. The inadequacy or simply the gradual loss of the old story does not necessarily suppress the image. Many times the imagery will take up habitation in a new — though not necessarily better — story.[62] At other times, a sharp and surprising movement within a story irrevocably alters how we view the image: after Challenger, the image of an ugly blast against deep blue sky has become a lens through which most of us view the continuing story of space exploration.

One other point about this dynamic relationship between story and image is that it allows for the possibility of typology as an appropriate theological and homiletical interpretive device. Liberal theologians and proponents of the "spirit of the age" may be appalled that this particular cat is out of the bag *again*. But if *lex orandi* has any merit, recall that at the great Easter vigil, the image of water is appropriately aligned with the stories of creation, flood, exodus, Jordan, and our baptism into Christ. Within the ministry of the Word as well, the preacher may want to look for the multivalence of images in the ways they align themselves with a series of stories. Whether or not we choose to adopt such an approach to the interpretation of Scripture, we can at least be alert to the "typologies" that emerge within our stories of self, church, and world.[63]

60. Harned, *Images for Self-Recognition,* p. 155.

61. See Ramshaw-Schmidt, *Christ in Sacred Speech: The Meaning of Liturgical Language* (Philadelphia: Fortress Press, 1986), pp. 23ff.

62. Robert Bellah "discovered" a whole new habitation for a tangled skein of biblical imagery, for example, within American civil religion. See my "Civil Religion and the Year of Grace," *Worship* 58 (July 1984): 372-83.

63. For a description of interacting image grids and suggestions of how to incorporate them within the sermon, see David Buttrick, *Homiletic,* pp. 163-70,

The integration of story and image within a single hermeneutic field also encourages a reconsideration of the notion of "point of view." Point of view is ordinarily discovered within the framework of the story and is employed within literary criticism "to designate the position or perspective from which a story is told."[64] However, the variety of points of view within biblical narrative serves to create a sense of unity as well as multi-dimensionality. "The resulting narrative is one with depth and sophistication," writes Adele Berlin, "one in which conflicting viewpoints may vie for validity. It is this that gives biblical narrative interest and ambiguity. The reader of such narrative is not a passive recipient of a story, but an active participant in trying to understand it."[65] Preachers who adopt narrative homiletic strategies will need to attend to point of view with great care. Out of control, point of view can create chaos within a congregational consciousness. A well-told narrative sermon will heed Berlin's insights and exploit them.

As image and story intersect, the possibilities associated with point of view expand dramatically for the interpreter and the preacher. The perception of images is inconceivable without the dimension of point of view. Even dreams and hallucinations involve some point of view, while images recollected under hypnosis are often characterized by a special vividness and a strong sense of "location" — which is to say, a clearly defined point of view. In light of this organic relationship between image and point of view, several observations of homiletical relevance may be noted:

1. Our point of view in perceiving an image is intimately connected with its affective impact on us. The experience of holding an infant, for example, is all bound up with point of view — tucking one's chin down, smiling into its close-held face, and so on.
2. Point of view also has implications for issues of theological value. Following Crossan's interpretation of the Parable of the Mustard Seed, we will look up toward triumphalist images of power and glory, but we will awkwardly peer down at this mustard-shrub parody of Israel's "Great Tree."[66]

64. Adele Berlin, *Poetics and Interpretation of Biblical Narrative* (Sheffield: Alword Press, 1983), p. 46. For an extensive study of point of view within biblical narrative, see pp. 43-82.
65. Berlin, *Poetics and Interpretation of Biblical Narrative*, p. 82.
66. See John Dominic Crossan, *In Parables: The Challenge of the Historical Jesus* (New York: Harper & Row, 1973), pp. 45-52.

3. In the case of verbal images, point of view may serve to invite the dynamic of transformation found within the biblical story. For example, the story of the man born blind in John 9 presents four distinct images of Christ from the perspective of the healed man. Beginning with an image of vague absence ("Where is he?" — "I do not know," v. 12), the story reaches its climax with a very different point of view: "Lord, I believe" (v. 38).[67]

Clearly point of view is a key element within the narrative structure. It can make the difference between confusion and awesome power in oral communication. As rhetoric once more reclaims its role within the field of homiletics, it will stress the role of point of view with respect to both image and story.

Finally, we will need to be reminded that as we encounter story and image, we struggle against the principalities and powers, the rulers of this age. These powers, too, have proved adept in employing stories and images; the world exploited this hermeneutic ellipsis before the church caught on. As Thomas Troeger notes, "Watching television conditions us to a way of knowing reality which operates not only through reason and principle, but through the capacities of the imagination to identify with vivid images and narratives of human life."[68] He goes on to contend that "the authority of effective preaching lies in the imaginative presentation of the gospel as a compelling alternative vision to the myths of the media."[69] In the midst of the myths of the media and the stories and images of a fallen world, God speaks the Word made flesh, revealed among us.

67. For an extensive study of the function of point of view within biblical narrative, see R. Alan Culpepper, *Anatomy of the Fourth Gospel: A Study in Literary Design* (Philadelphia: Fortress Press, 1983), pp. 15ff.

68. Troeger, "Imaginative Theology: The Shape of Post-Modern Homiletics," *Homiletic* 13 (1988): 31.

69. Troeger, "Imaginative Theology," p. 31.

On Doing Homiletics Today

David Buttrick

The ragged end of the twentieth century is a moment of change; we live between the times. Rather obviously, the intellectual construct of the Enlightenment has collapsed. Is not "post-modern" a vogue term of late? Certainly we have seen paradigm shifts in most fields of human endeavor. So anyone who would do homiletics is struggling in the midst of what might be termed an intellectual guessing game. The homiletic wisdom of fifty years ago is no longer sure, the languages we speak are changing, and some common "cultural formulation" is still unformed.[1] So, these days we grope not only for methodology but for some new theoretical basis for homiletics in philosophical theology, which itself seems to be searching for renewal. Local preachers who quite properly crave clear procedures are confused: Do we speak inductively, "tell our stories," paint images, or what?[2] The church's evangelical mandate is still compelling; the gospel must be preached. The question is How?

---

1. I borrow the term "cultural formulation" from Crane Brinton, who uses it to describe the constellation of beliefs (often tacit) that a given cultural epoch affirms. See his *History of Western Morals* (New York: Harcourt, Brace, 1959).
2. Elizabeth Achtemeier has written of the confusion in homiletics in "The Artful Dialogue," *Interpretation* 35 (January 1981): 18-31; and Richard L. Eslinger has discussed major alternatives in *A New Hearing: Living Options in Homiletic Method* (Nashville: Abingdon Press, 1987).

"The Times They Are A-changing"

Preaching in any age is a complicated task. For preaching is not only a hermeneutic activity of reading texts and human situations; it involves shaping words with rhetorical savvy to form understandings in common consciousness. The homiletic task involves the informed study of Scripture, theological reflection, cultural analysis, and hard-nosed rhetorical craft. Any homiletician must be alert to intellectual shifts that are taking place in a number of fields.

Let us line out some of these changes.

Biblical Scholarship

For nearly two hundred years, historical-critical method has been in vogue. Though it began as "Scientific Method," posing as objective procedure, it was soon buttressed by notions of historical revelation proposed by the biblical theology movement. But recently one biblical scholar baldly announced that "historical biblical criticism is bankrupt,"[3] and another has detailed the "slow dissolution" of the biblical theology movement.[4] These days there are a number of new methodologies — structuralist, reader-response, sociological, psychological, deconstructionist, rhetorical, phenomenological, and more.[5]

The problem can be seen rather clearly with reference to the parables of Jesus. In the 1890s, the great Adolf Jülicher, working with historical-critical procedures, argued against the usual allegorical interpretation of parables; he insisted that parables are stories of everyday life in Palestine and are essentially simple comparisons with single meanings — A is *like* B.[6] While scholars subsequently corrected Jülicher's somewhat

---

3. Walter Wink, *The Bible in Human Transformation* (Philadelphia: Fortress, 1973), p. 1.

4. Brevard S. Childs, *Biblical Theology in Crisis* (Philadelphia: Westminster Press, 1970), p. 87.

5. See a catalogue of several proposals in Edgar V. McKnight, *The Bible and the Reader* (Philadelphia: Fortress, 1985).

6. See Jülicher, *Die Gleichnisreden Jesu* (Darmstadt: Wissenschaftliche Buchgesellschaft, 1963). For a discussion of Jülicher's notion of a single, simple comparison, see chap. 5 of Robert W. Funk's *Language, Hermeneutic and Word of God* (New York: Harper & Row, 1966).

naive theological liberalism by recognizing Jewish precedents and by admitting eschatological dimension, the historical paradigm held.[7] Preachers interpreted parables by reading them in their first-century setting and then grasping the essential teachings they contained. But then, in 1972, participants in the Society for Biblical Literature Parables Seminar took a second look at the parables of Jesus using different literary-critical approaches, and suddenly the parables seemed to change.[8] We realized that both of Jülicher's assumptions were unsure: parables were frequently "surreal" and not merely mirrors of everyday life in Palestine. What's more, parables did not propose single "teachings" but were systems of language characterized by movement that could work transformations in the consciousness of listeners.[9]

Obviously a traditional homiletic that distilled topics from texts, "lessons" to be preached, could work with Jülicher's assumptions; a single meaning could be distilled and points made. But, just as obviously, traditional homiletics might have difficulty handling "traveling" systems of language, not to mention surreal "Brechtian" exaggerations intended to disrupt our "world" in consciousness.[10]

A similar scenario could be sketched for other types of biblical literature. While no one would wish to deny the wealth of wisdom gleaned from Scripture by historical-critical method, it is nevertheless the case that preachers do not preach *about* the Bible; they declare the gospel *of* the Bible. A rational homiletic designed for the presentation of distilled "truths" and "teachings" from historical texts simply cannot cope with emerging new forms of biblical criticism. Any homiletic that would serve the future must align with the various literary critical options now being practiced.

7. For a history of subsequent parable interpretation, see G. V. Jones, *The Art and Truth of the Parables* (London: S.P.C.K., 1964), pp. 3-54.

8. See chap. 3 of Norman Perrin's *Jesus and the Language of the Kingdom* (Philadelphia: Fortress Press, 1976).

9. See my article "On Preaching a Parable: The Problem of Homiletic Method," *Reformed Liturgy and Music* 17 (Winter 1983): 16-22. Recent literature on parables is extensive, but I have learned much from Bernard Brandon Scott's *Hear Then the Parable* (Philadelphia: Fortress Press, 1989).

10. Brecht spoke of *Verfremdungseffekt* ("alienation effects"), by which he meant devices employed to disrupt an audience's identification with dramatic characters so as to prevent catharsis. He regarded catharsis as a block to revolutionary change. See *Brecht on Theatre*, ed. and trans. John Willett (New York: Hill & Wang, 1966).

Theological Revision

If biblical criticism appears to be undergoing a paradigm shift, so also is the theological enterprise.[11] Scholars in America — notably Edward Farley, Francis Schüssler Fiorenza, and David Tracy — are moving theology from traditional foundations; they are not only challenging methodological conventions but proposing structures of thought that clearly break with the ruling neo-orthodoxy that has been with us for half a century.[12]

Two matters may be cited. First, the rise of hermeneutic literature in the past quarter-century has had enormous impact on all the theological disciplines. Certainly the work of Paul Ricoeur has undercut rationalist notions of the objective witness of Scripture,[13] and the edgy analysis of the Frankfurt School's "Critical Theory" has made us wary of our supposedly "objective" historical-critical scholarship.[14] Now a growing literature from Liberation Theology is challenging the predominant European/masculine/Protestant tradition of interpretation.[15] Obviously conventional notions of biblical authority — a homiletic "stock-in-trade" — are no longer tenable.[16] The second shift in contemporary theology has occurred under the rubric "Revelation." For the most part, neo-orthodoxy, refusing "natural theology" and rejecting Schleiermacher, looked for revelation in history. Neo-orthodox theologians supposed that the sovereign God has

11. See part 1 of David Tracy's *Blessed Rage for Order* (New York: Seabury Press, 1975).

12. I have in mind, e.g., Farley's *Ecclesial Man* (Philadelphia: Fortress Press, 1975) and *Ecclesial Reflection* (Philadelphia: Fortress Press, 1982); Fiorenza's *Foundational Theology* (New York: Crossroad, 1985); and Tracy's *Analogical Imagination* (New York: Crossroad, 1981).

13. For a fairly accessible presentation of Ricoeur's biblical hermeneutics, see *Semeia 4: Paul Ricoeur on Biblical Hermeneutics,* ed. J. D. Crossan (Missoula, Mont.: Scholars Press, 1975), which contains "Biblical Hermeneutics," an extended essay by Ricoeur, plus a helpful introduction by Loretta Dornish. For a concise presentation of Ricoeur's theory, see his *Interpretation Theory: Discourse and the Surplus of Meaning* (Fort Worth: Texas Christian University Press, 1976).

14. On Critical Theory, see the discussion by David Held in *Introduction to Critical Theory: Horkeimer to Habermas* (Berkeley and Los Angeles: University of California Press, 1980).

15. See "Biblical Hermeneutics in the Theologies of Liberation," in *Irruption of the Third World: Challenge to Theology,* ed. Virginia Fabella and Sergio Torres (Maryknoll, N.Y.: Orbis Books, 1983), pp. 140-68.

16. See chap. 15 of my *Homiletic* (Philadelphia: Fortress Press, 1987). For a much more important treatment, see part 1 of Edward Farley's *Ecclesial Reflection.*

been self-disclosed in "mighty acts" of "salvation history."[17] Of late, there
has been a decided shift from the historical model and at the same time
a turn toward notions of revelation connected with symbol and social
consciousness.[18] Inasmuch as preaching has been obsessed with the historical paradigm, this shift appears to call for a wholesale reconception of
the preaching task. If a nineteenth-century concern for the relationship
between revelation and consciousness is being rehabilitated, a homiletics
concerned with consciousness, and specifically with language in consciousness, may be required.

Further, what goes on in philosophical theology always ends up in
homiletics. Just as rhetoric and philosophy have played tag through the
ages, so have theology and homiletics. In our century, however, that
relationship has been disrupted. During the rise of the biblical theology
movement, a fickle homiletics began to dally with biblical studies, to regard
itself as a consort of biblical fields. Now, once again, homiletics will have
to rethink itself in relation to the quite radical reformulations that are
beginning to take place in the theological disciplines.

Cultural Formulation

How are we to get at changes happening in the human world? Shall we
point to the rise of so-called Third and Fourth World peoples? Certainly
we must expect that formative centers of future thought will be in Asia
and Africa. Or shall we detail the sudden emergence of esoteric technology
in space physics and computer logic? No, to get at the human social
situation, we must trace wider patterns in the public mind.

Can we not point to what might be termed "high periods" in
cultural history? Such periods are marked by synthesis between religion
and cultural formulation, a weaving of what Peter Berger has labeled "the

17. James Barr has suggested that "historians of theology in a future age will look
back on the mid-twentieth century and call it the revelation-in-history period" ("Revelation
through History in the Old Testament and in Modern Theology," in *New Theology No. 1,*
ed. Martin E. Marty and Dean G. Peerman [New York: Macmillan, 1964], p. 60). The
position associated with biblical scholars such as G. Ernest Wright, Gerhard von Rad, and
Oscar Cullmann is articulated by John Baillie in *The Idea of Revelation in Recent Thought*
(New York: Columbia University Press, 1956).

18. See, e.g., part 2, chap. 9 of Avery Dulles's *Models of Revelation* (Garden City,
N.Y.: Doubleday, 1983).

sacred canopy."[19] The medieval synthesis was defined by the analogy between the heavenly "City of God" and the "city" of the church in the world, as well as by an *analogia entis* between the nature of God and human nature.[20] A similar synthesis in the eighteenth century was marked by an analogy between the divine rationality perceived in the patterns of nature and the rational capacities of human beings.[21] In "high periods," most people share the same synthetic convictions; there is little tension between cultural assumptions and general religious conviction. There are set social patterns, linguistic stability, and common rhetorical conventions. In such eras, "vertical" piety is widespread, and religious conversion is understood as alignment with the fixity of God's glory — in effect, we "get right" with God. A sense of transcendence animates the age and shows up in expectations of immortality. Eugène Ionesco captures the mood when he presents his "hero" Bérenger roaming a world of utopian Idealism:

> Gardens, blue sky, or the spring which corresponds to the universe inside . . . or a mirror in which its own smile could be reflected . . . a smiling being in a smiling world. . . . I felt I could go on living, and yet I couldn't die.[22]

By contrast, we can also spot eras marked by social dissolution, times that may be described as cultural "breakdowns." Such breakdowns are marked by rising conflict between a fragmenting cultural formulation and radically dialectical religious thought; synthesis gives way to sharp tensions. In such eras — think of the collapse of the Greco-Roman world, the dissolution of the medieval synthesis, and the mid-twentieth century — language, after shrinking defensively, suddenly multiplies,[23] common

---

19. Berger, *The Sacred Canopy: Elements of a Sociological Theory of Religion* (Garden City, N.Y.: Doubleday, 1967).

20. On this, see Jaroslav Pelikan, *The Christian Tradition: A History of the Development of Doctrine*, vol. 3: *The Growth of Medieval Theology (600-1300)* (Chicago: University of Chicago Press, 1978), 293-307.

21. See Carl L. Becker, *The Heavenly City of the Eighteenth-Century Philosophers* (New Haven: Yale University Press, 1932).

22. Ionesco, *The Killer and Other Plays* (New York: Grove Press, 1960), p. 19. In the same speech, Bérenger complains, "When there's not a total agreement between myself inside and myself outside, then it's a catastrophe, a universal contradiction, a schism." Later he discovers a fountain filled with throat-cut corpses, and his radiant romantic "city" vanishes.

23. See Dwight Macdonald, "The String Untuned," *The New Yorker,* 10 March 1962.

metaphors are hard to come by, and the sense of analogy dissolves or becomes at best a "negative analogy" — for example, the hollow-souled sculptures of Henry Moore standing in the presence of *Deus Absconditus.* Vertical piety is difficult to maintain, and conversion, if credited at all, involves a kind of journeying. Ideas of immortality fade, and once more human beings face the immense, stern fact of dying.[24] No wonder the dialectical theology of Karl Barth appeared in the middle of the twentieth century, denying *analogia entis,* deposing "natural theology," and asserting an objective biblical witness over against all cultural wisdoms: Christian faith was seeking to disengage from a collapsing cultural formulation.

Now, as almost any social analyst admits, we live "between the times." Periods of social collapse and redefinition (if such occurs) may take decades or even centuries, as countercultural oppositions turn around to become some sort of new formulation.[25] It is in such a moment that we are trying to do homiletics. Though the Barthian dialectic is still an option, more and more it must be regarded as a reactionary posture.[26] Somehow homiletic thought must venture, must probe the new language now forming in the world, must seek to re-image theological meaning beyond the biblical page, must once more attempt to assemble a "sacred rhetoric" that can be evangelically useful in a re-forming human world.

Gesturing a New Homiletic

What kind of homiletic do we frame for the forming new age? The question is exceedingly difficult to answer. Let us wave toward some concerns that may be crucial.[27]

---

24. Frederick Hoffman insists that the twentieth century has rediscovered the fact of death, which had been hidden in soft folds of Victorian sentimentality; see *The Mortal No: Death and the Modern Imagination* (Princeton: Princeton University Press, 1984).

25. Drawing on the work of anthropologist Anthony F. C. Wallace, William G. McLaughlin suggests a sequential pattern involved in cultural breakdowns and renewals in chap. 1 of *Revivals, Awakenings, and Reform* (Chicago: University of Chicago Press, 1978).

26. See my analysis of this point in "Preaching in an *Un*brave New World," *The (Vanderbilt University Divinity School) Spire* 13 (Summer/Fall 1988).

27. In the following discussions, I draw from my very tentative attempt to formulate a new homiletic, *Homiletic.*

The Concept of Plot

Enlightenment homiletics inherited a three-phased sacred rhetoric from Protestant Scholastics involving *subtilitas intelligendi, subtilitas explicandi,* and *subtilitas applicandi:* texts were understood exegetically, explicated theologically, and then applied. In the nineteenth century, that pattern was reduced in no small part because the church was embarrassed by features of the biblical text — after David Hume, miracles were troubling, and, in the midst of elevated romantic idealism, the earthiness of the Hebrew scriptures was often a source of dismay. So exegesis was reduced to historical reconstruction, theological interpretation was transformed into a search for "topical themes," and application expanded into multiple "points" that were often developed categorically. As Hans Frei observed, the narrative structure of Scripture was lost.[28] Homiletics busied itself with "eternal truths" detached from the messy, often troubling details of Scripture. Please note: during cultural "highs," sermons tend to be deductive, elaborations of the holy, fixed truths of God.

But recent biblical research, involving literary critical approaches or structuralist exegesis, has restored an appreciation for narrative sequence, for the structural design and moving logic of pericopes. We are beginning to see that Scripture is made up of plotted stories rather than hi*story.*[29] Even in non-narrative passages, the language of Scripture seems to involve a traveling "scenario" of ideas.[30] Biblical language is not analogous to a still-life picture from which an objective viewer may select some item as a topic for discussion; it is much more like a film clip that, in a moving sequence, makes meaning happen.[31] If, in fact, biblical language is "plotted" by the interaction between an intentional writer and the intersubjective consciousness of an intended audience, the presumably homiletic design could embrace a similar procedure in its strategic presentations.

28. Frei, *The Eclipse of Biblical Narrative: A Study in Eighteenth and Nineteenth Century Hermeneutics* (New Haven: Yale University Press, 1974).

29. E. M. Forster was one of the first literary critics to describe a distinction between plot and history; see chap. 2 of his *Aspects of the Novel* (New York: Harcourt, Brace & World, 1927).

30. I do not embrace the notion that preaching should tell stories because the gospel is essentially a "story." The language of faith is a "horizontal" narrativity, but it is also "vertical" symbolic-reflective language that grasps symbols within the hermeneutic of a "being-saved community." Thus, I stress the notion of plotted mobility rather than narrativity. See chap. 1 of my *Homiletic.*

31. See my argument in "Interpretation and Preaching," *Interpretation* 35 (January 1981): 46-58.

Some observations may be ventured on the subject of "plot":

1. Traditionally, much preaching has involved what might be described as "third-person observational language." We have looked at, talked about, and pointed to things, events, and ideas; we have employed an objective rationalist rhetoric that "makes points." But in ordinary conversation these days, people employ various points of view; they speak from different attitudes and perspectives, and they shift around as they speak. The difference between what we have termed the rationalist perspective and the relative friskiness of ordinary language is analogous to the difference in filmmaking between an old-fashioned fixed camera trained on actors in a static shot and contemporary cameras that move on tracks and cranes to capture a scene from many changing angles of vision.[32] Contemporary fiction, much contemporary art, and even contemporary theology have acknowledged the relativity of human consciousness these days, a relativity expressed in points of view.[33] A mobile sermon design permits the introduction of changing points of view that may match the shifting perspectives of human consciousness quite naturally.

2. As Chaim Perelman has observed, rhetoric has been captive to rational philosophical logic that has moved it away from the kinds of paralogic native to human consciousness — logics that are, of course, much closer to patterns of biblical thought.[34] The Bible seems to "think" in narrative, in images and analogies, in ritual symbols and communal recollections.[35] The concept of plot enables us to design a movement of thought that is strung together by a logic of consciousness rather than by patterns of deductive reasoning. Thus, the "moves" in a sermon's movement assemble by association, by analogy, by contrast, and the like; they may form a plotted sequence designed to match typical modes of human consciousness.[36] The concept of plot also allows for disruptions or reversals in thought in a way that usual homiletic design does not. If, for example,

---

32. I explore this point further in chap. 4 of *Homiletic*.

33. Langdon Gilkey offers a fine analysis of contemporary relativism in chap. 2 of *Naming the Whirlwind: The Renewal of God-Language* (New York: Bobbs-Merrill, 1969).

34. See Perelman, *The Realm of Rhetoric,* trans. W. Kluback (Notre Dame, Ind.: University of Notre Dame Press, 1982).

35. For some fascinating studies of the subtle logic involved in biblical narratives, see Robert Alter, *The Art of Biblical Narrative* (New York: Basic Books, 1981).

36. For an analysis of different logics of consciousness, see Chaim Perelman and L. Olbrechts-Tyteca, *The New Rhetoric: A Treatise on Argumentation,* trans. J. Wilkinson and P. Weaver (Notre Dame, Ind.: University of Notre Dame Press, 1969).

some parables "frustrate our expectations"[37] in surprising ways, a system of "moves" permits the intrusion of the unexpected into a sequence of thought.

Above all, the notion of plot matches the "style" of our cultural moment: we live in transition, journeying. Do we not chatter about "narrative theology" and "process theology" of late? During cultural "highs," thought is apt to be vertical and static, but ours is a time of cultural movement, of breakdown and reassembly, in which a whole world seems to be "changing its mind." Temporality has once more invaded the cultural mind, and with it forms of apocalyptic eschatology. Sermons in an age such as ours cannot be "vertically" deductive; they must move, journeying toward understanding.

Moments of Consciousness

Traditional homiletics tended to catalogue sermons according to either purpose or subject matter. While these categories were obviously true and useful, they scarcely related to matters of form and style. If sermons are designed to match natural patterns of human consciousness, we may have to employ a very different sort of typology. I have elsewhere suggested the analogy of an art gallery.[38] In such a context, I can gaze at a painting and experience the immediate force of its composition in consciousness. Later I can recall and reconsider the painting at a distance. With the painting in the back of my mind, I can go out into the world and regard things quite differently — through new vision supplied by the painting. These moments in consciousness relate to different types of sermon design and, in fact, may issue in different rhetorical styles. For example, the sophisticated plot lines of some parables may require a sermon design that moves with immediate controlling force in attendant consciousness — a sermon strategy designed to *do,* because parables may well be a language of conversion. By contrast, a Pauline passage may well produce sermons designed to match a kind of "distant mnemonic reflec-

37. Wolfgang Iser uses the phrase "frustrate our expectations" and describes the process in chap. 8 of *The Act of Reading: A Theory of Aesthetic Response* (Baltimore: The Johns Hopkins University Press, 1978). Iser seems to be influenced by the literary theory of Umberto Eco.

38. See chap. 20 of my *Homiletic.*

tion." And are there not sermons that view the world in a worldly way but with the transforming vision of the gospel in the back of our minds? The language of preaching may thus be related to different moments in consciousness.

What I do *not* find useful is the notion that we preach from Scripture in any direct way. In recent years, a number of books have promoted a kind of biblical preaching that purports to trace a process of preparation from exegesis to sermon.[39] If you look these books over, you discover that they offer a detailed program for exegesis and an equally detailed set of homiletic procedures; what they do not do is explain what happens in between the two activities — namely, the leap of imagination that moves from the biblical text to a basic sermon design. An older homiletics could be specific: begin with a given topic, choose a single verse as text, make assorted points, and so on. Alternatively, as we study the structure of a scriptural passage, we may form an analogous structure of contemporary meaning in consciousness, a structure that, in fact, *does* design our sermons.[40] This intermediate structure of consciousness is, of course, an act of contemporary theological understanding that in turn enables us to determine the components of our sermon design. Thus, there is some proper relationship between the structural components of a text and the moves of a sermon "scenario."[41]

Intentionality and Preaching

A number of years ago William Wimsatt Jr. wrote an article on what he labeled the "intentional fallacy."[42] He insisted that literary critics can rightly make no judgment with regard to an author's purpose. Few

39. Among New Testament scholars, see, e.g., Reginald H. Fuller, *The Use of the Bible in Preaching* (Philadelphia: Fortress Press, 1981), and Ernest Best, *From Text to Sermon* (Atlanta: John Knox Press, 1978); among homileticians, see James Cox, *A Guide to Biblical Preaching* (Nashville: Abingdon Press, 1976), and William D. Thompson, *Preaching Biblically* (Nashville: Abingdon Press, 1981).

40. Buttrick, *Homiletic,* pp. 308-9.

41. Ever since the publication of Amos Wilder's *Language of the Gospel: Early Christian Rhetoric* (London: SCM Press, 1964), homileticians have speculated that there is some sort of connection between biblical forms and sermon design. For a helpful recent study, see Thomas G. Long, *Preaching and the Literary Forms of the Bible* (Philadelphia: Fortress Press, 1988)

42. See Wimsatt, *The Verbal Icon* (New York: Noonday Press, 1962), p. 18.

scholars these days would be inclined to tangle with Wimsatt on this point.[43] When we interpret biblical texts, we are seldom so tempted, because in most cases we haven't the foggiest notion of who the author might be. Nevertheless, can we not speak of an intending in the *language* itself? Rhetoricians have long argued that an implied audience may be deduced from reading a political address. The reverse is also true; an implied authorial strategist may be equally apparent. So, let us propose that biblical language is intentional and, therefore, in some sense preformative. We can explore the proposition by looking at the little parable in Luke 17:7-10.

> [7]Suppose you have a slave ploughing or tending livestock: when he comes in from the field, will you say to him, "Come and relax at table"? [8]Rather, will [you] not say to him, "Get me my supper, and dress to wait on me while I eat and drink. After that, you can eat and drink"? [9]Would [you] thank the slave because he does what he's told to do? No! [10]So you, when you do everything you are told to do, say, "We are unworthy slaves; we are only doing what we're supposed to do."[44]

Notice that in verses 7-9, listeners are placed in the position of mastery, whereas suddenly, in verse 10, they find themselves dumped unceremoniously into the position of a mere laborer. The question: Is the intending-to-do action of the parable part of its meaning? If it is, then preaching must find some way to replicate the demoting action of the parable in the structure of a sermon.

The example above is actually quite simple; it demonstrates a single intentional *action*. Most pericopes are far more sophisticated. Let us glance at another brief example, proposed by John Dominic Crossan.[45]

> [38]You have heard that it was said, "An eye for any eye and a tooth for a tooth." [39]But I'm telling you, do not oppose evil. But if anyone

---

43. Although see chap. 1 of E. D. Hirsch Jr.'s *Validity in Interpretation* (New Haven: Yale University Press, 1967).

44. My translation. Note that I have twice replaced the masculine pronoun with a bracketed *[you]*; some scholars suppose that, in view of v. 7, "you" may have been a feature of the original "scenario."

45. See Crossan, *Raid on the Articulate: Comic Eschatology in Jesus and Borges* (New York: Harper & Row, 1976), pp. 63-69. Crossan gathers evidence to establish a case law form and then argues that the language of Jesus is a deliberate "case parody."

smacks you on the right cheek, turn to him the other as well; [40]if anyone takes your shirt in a lawsuit, let him have your topcoat as well; [41]and if anyone commandeers you for one mile, go two for him.[46]

The structural design of the passage may well be rabbinic: there is the quotation of the famous *ius talionis* from Exodus 21:24, the articulation of a sweeping general rubric ("Do not oppose evil"), and, finally, three "case law" examples that are similar in form to the collected case law offered in Exodus 20:22–23:33. The "If . . . then . . ." form permits casuistic exceptions to a general rule. We may assume that the original audience (possibly Pharisees) was not only familiar with case law form but, after a sweeping rule such as "do not oppose evil," was positively eager for some sane exceptions — as, indeed, we all may be! But, instead of exceptions, in each case the general rule is extravagantly reinforced. The pericope is a call to radical love.

Again, our question: Isn't the structural action of the pericope part of its meaning? Should not a sermon on the passage intend toward our compulsion to ease the demands of our faith and then, somehow, shatter our expectations with radical examples drawn from our *contemporary* world? The pericope is intentionally complex: it seeks to bring out the "much more" of God's demands, to address our timid desires for moderation, and then to reinforce the absolutely radical character of Christian love. Obviously an "objective" discussion of the passage will not suffice; somehow the passage must *do*.

I am suggesting that in the present cultural moment homiletics will feature mobile "plots" and a concern for intentional purpose.[47] Further, I am suggesting that the structural "shape" of pericopes can relate to structures of contemporary meaning in consciousness. Though we need not (and possibly should not) replicate the particular sequence of a passage in our sermons, we will tend to employ structural components of meaning found in a passage in the "moves" of some newly "plotted" sermon design.

---

46. Matt. 5:38-41, my translation. Note that in Luke the pattern of verse 40 is humorously reversed: if anyone takes your outergarment, give him your undergarment as well.

47. For a more detailed discussion of plot and intention, see chap. 18 of my *Homiletic*.

Theological Footwork

A Social Hermeneutic

When the so-called "New Hermeneutic" was proposed in the 1960s by post-Bultmannians Ernst Fuchs and Gerhard Ebeling, it had an enormous impact on homiletic theory.[48] Yet the movement came and went with startling dispatch. Probably the fatal flaw was a lurking assumption — namely, that the gospel addresses human beings in their existential self-awareness.[49] This rendered the model inescapably personalist, and as a result, particularly in America, it was assimilated into what Philip Rieff has labeled "the triumph of the therapeutic."[50] Of course, the problem is not uniquely American; leftover nineteenth-century pietism met a rising interest in psychoanalytic thought in the early twentieth century to create pulpit "personalism" almost everywhere — *except*, please note, among the oppressed.[51] Of course, pulpit personalism may be a form of romantic evasion at a time when we are all becoming much more aware of our captivities to the social "powers that be."[52]

The problem with the "new hermeneutic" was not so much infidelity to Scripture, as some Barthians supposed, but an existentialist bent (aligned with Lutheran piety?) that overlooked human intersubjectivity. A new homiletic will have to acknowledge what might be termed the "social hermeneutic" of the gospel. Obviously human beings do live in "me/myself" awareness. What's more, preaching salvation is bound to include a promise of liberation from psychological structures that deform and inhibit a fine, free life before God. Nevertheless, Scripture seems to be addressed to a shared social consciousness — indeed, a *communal* consciousness shaped by religious images and symbols — and not to random individuals in existential self-awareness. Moreover, as collective forms of the demonic more and more

---

48. See *The New Hermeneutic,* ed. J. M. Robinson and J. B. Cobb Jr. (New York: Harper & Row, 1964). For a careful analysis of the movement, see Paul J. Achtemeier, *Introduction to the New Hermeneutic* (Philadelphia: Westminster Press, 1969).

49. Such an assumption may still undergird the work of a brilliant homiletician, Fred B. Craddock; see chap. 5 of his book *Preaching* (Nashville: Abingdon Press, 1985).

50. See Rieff, *The Triumph of the Therapeutic: Uses of Faith after Freud* (New York: Harper & Row, 1966).

51. See my discussion of Harry Emerson Fosdick's sermons in "Preaching in an Unbrave New World."

52. See Walter Wink's two volumes, *Naming the Powers* (Philadelphia: Fortress Press, 1984) and *Unmasking the Powers* (Philadelphia: Fortress Press, 1986).

shadow our lives, if we are to preach salvation, we must pose promises of social liberation that extend beyond the usual models of personal conversion.[53] To do so, we must develop a hermeneutic that is savvy concerning both the intersubjective nature of human consciousness and those symbolic structures of common life signaled by sociologies of knowledge.[54]

The Phenomenology of Language

Homiletics has not always been aware of its philosophical alliances; it has often indiscriminately picked up unexamined strands of cultural thought and formulations. These days we find homiletic theory shaped by structuralism, eschatological theologies, theories of narrativity, Wittgensteinian linguistics, and goodness know what else. But, because preachers speak, homiletics ought to work from some sort of studied understanding of language.

The issue can be pinpointed: *Any theory of language we embrace must acknowledge the social character of language and yet allow for the possibility of revelation through language.* While much contemporary communications theory does recognize the social character of language, it does not permit any openness to transcendence; after all, communications theory emerged from analytical philosophy that conceived of language as empirically referential as well as a medium of rational exchange. Likewise, sophistications of general linguistics since Ferdinand de Saussure, though aware of the depth of human conceptualization, do not seem to leave much room for the possibility of revelation.[55]

But clearly there are resources in the later Heidegger[56] and also in

---

53. See chap. 4 of my *Preaching Jesus Christ: An Exercise in Homiletic Theology* (Philadelphia: Fortress Press, 1987).

54. Here I refer to the work of Alfred Schutz, *The Phenomenology of the Social World* (Evanston, Ill.: Northwestern University Press, 1967) and *The Structures of the Life World* (Evanston, Ill.: Northwestern University Press, 1973), and also to the collaborative work of Schutz disciples Peter L. Berger and Thomas Luckmann, *The Social Construction of Reality* (Garden City, N.Y.: Doubleday, 1967).

55. It seems to me that Ricoeur's critique of the structuralist enterprise is still essentially correct; see the three essays in part 1 of his *Conflict of Interpretations: Essays in Hermeneutics* (Evanston, Ill.: Northwestern University Press, 1974).

56. In particular, Heidegger's *What Is Called Thinking?* trans. J. Glenn Gray and Fred D. Wieck (New York: Harper & Row, 1972), *On the Way to Language* (New York: Harper & Row, 1982), and *Poetry, Language, Thought,* trans. Albert Hofstadter (New York: Harper & Row, 1975).

continental phenomenologies of language[57] that offer homiletic theory some basis for formulation. Certainly Heidegger affirms that language can bring out disclosures of Being. And phenomenologies of language affirm that language shapes the world-in-consciousness, locates and identifies the self-in-the-world, and builds eschatological vision to direct our steps. Preaching obviously intends to constitute a faith-world and to disclose the awesome Presence-in-absence of God-with-us. Thus preaching involves language and communal consciousness. It seems to me that homiletic theory can be at home in an understanding of language informed by social phenomenologies.

Preaching and Revelation

I have suggested that homiletics since the mid-twentieth century has been captive to a now-passé biblical theology movement — as witness a number of homiletic works that propose preaching (1) as *recital* or (2) as a secondary *witness to Scripture*.[58] In the one case, preaching brings to contemporary congregations "mighty acts of God," reconstituting a "salvation history" of revelatory events; basically preaching is understood as a transmission of past disclosures to the present day. The other model is more vertical and is radically Christocentric: God is a self-revealer; God's self-revelation is Jesus Christ; Scripture is the objective witness to Christ; and, in turn, preaching is witness to the witness of Scripture. Though Barth wrote more about preaching than any other modern theologian, ultimately the Barthian model seems to undercut the living power of the Word; preaching is reduced to a transmission of the past.

But if our models of revelation change, if we conceive of God as not so much an actor in history but a symbol-giver to human social consciousness,[59] then the role of preaching will be redefined. We will once

57. I have in mind here the work of Maurice Merleau-Ponty as well as the work of those who have been influenced by him — G. Gusdorf, *Speaking* (Evanston, Ill.: Northwestern University Press, 1965), and R. Kwant, *Phenomenology of Language* (Pittsburgh: Duquesne University Press, 1965).

58. See, e.g., the early work by D. Ritchel, *A Theology of Proclamation* (Richmond: John Knox Press, 1960), and Jean-Jacques von Allmen's *Preaching and Congregation* (Richmond: John Knox, 1962).

59. See a splendid essay by Edward Farley, "God as Dominator and Image-Giver: Divine Sovereignty and the New Anthropology," *Journal of Ecumenical Studies* 6 (1969): 354-75.

more affirm Luther's strong sense of preaching as a present-tense "Word of God." St. Paul shouts out, "*Now* is the day of salvation!" (2 Cor. 6:2). Preaching lives in the "now" of salvation. So, in the present tense, preaching will once more name God in the world, form faith, address human situations, construct powerful eschatological vision, and, indeed, announce God's New Order, what Jesus called "the kingdom of God."[60]

Homiletics can emerge from the objective/subjective split in which it has been trapped — either objectively rational or subjectively romantic — by moving toward the notion of consciousness where objective and subjective meet. More, homiletics can find a home in models of revelation that relate to images and symbols in social consciousness. The doing of homiletics these days is complex but urgent. "Faith comes from hearing," says St. Paul (Rom. 10:17), therein providing the *raison d'être* for our homiletic energies.

60. There seems to be a pendulum swing between preaching the message of Jesus (viz., "the kingdom of God is at hand") and preaching a message about Jesus that can become triumphalist and in our time may have done so. Now, between the ages, we may have to recover the eschatological message of God's new order.

As One *with* Authority:
Rehabilitating Concepts for Preaching

David M. Greenhaw

The focus on the particular and concrete, characteristic of the inductive turn in preaching, has unwittingly fed a reluctance to proclaim the gospel with authority.[1] Carefully crafted stories, anecdotes, and vignettes are woven together in sermons, but the point of the telling is often lost. Far too much preaching today focuses on the particular at the expense of the universal and consequently fails to make real claims or exercise a legitimate authority.

The gospel cannot be proclaimed without authority. To preach the gospel of Jesus Christ, it is necessary to articulate claims on our lives boldly and announce what is new because of what God is doing. To do this, the preacher must move beyond the opacity of the particular to the clarity of the universal. It will not do to speak only of particulars, of what is true for me or true for this pericope. To preach, one must speak a truth that can transcend a particular setting. Until it is possible to transcend a particular setting, until some universal is approached, the gospel may be an interesting story or an enlightening account of some piece of history, but it lacks the power to transform. Before gospel truth can transform

---

1. With the publication of Fred Craddock's *As One without Authority* (Nashville: Abingdon Press, 1971), homiletic theory has become intensely interested in induction as a principal means of preaching. "Everyone lives inductively, not deductively," argues Craddock. "No farmer deals with the problem of calfhood, only with the calf. The woman in the kitchen is not occupied with the culinary arts in general but with a particular roast or cake" (p. 60).

human beings, the particularity of the gospel in one setting must be transferred through a universal to a new particularity.

When a sermon fails to move beyond the particular, when it fails to make a point out of the stories it tells, it reflects a paralysis of fear. Making a point, articulating a claim — this is dangerous stuff. The preacher could be wrong, and in being wrong might inflict harm on the hearers. There is always the possibility that what the preacher says is too conditioned by personal bias. One's preaching may have nothing to do with the gospel and everything to do with one's own idiosyncrasies or even neuroses. Such fears are appropriate; every preacher should be mindful of them on entering the pulpit. But it is also true that if one is to preach, one has to have something to say and has to say it boldly.[2]

A Change in Problematic

When a publication in the field of homiletics strikes a strong chord and is widely read, it is probably because the author's hunch about a problem in preaching has been accurate.[3] At least this was the case with Fred Craddock's *As One without Authority.* Since the publication of this book in 1971, a remarkable consensus has formed among homileticians that a "conceptual method" is not appropriate for preaching and that an inductive approach is preferable to a deductive approach.[4] Craddock struck a chord not simply because he offered a viable and convincing case for an inductive preaching method but because he defined a problem that needed

2. On the importance of having something to say in preaching, see my essay "Why Preach? Why Listen? Why Bother?" in *The (Vanderbilt University Divinity School) Spire* 13 (1988): 8.

3. There are no clearly defined and universally accepted indicators of the current state of preaching. While it is possible to follow trends in homiletic literature, there is little assurance that these trends reflect what is actually going on in Christian pulpits. Even published sermons are not wholly accurate indicators of the current state of preaching, since what is suitable for publication may not be suitable for oral presentation and vice versa. Hence it is difficult to say with any certainty exactly what sorts of problems are showing up in contemporary preaching. In sorting out the problems, we have to rely on educated hunches and anecdotal evidence.

4. For a review of the trends in the literature, see F. Wellford Hobbie, "The Play Is the Thing: New Forms for the Sermon," *Journal for Preachers* 5 (1982): 17-23.

addressing. As Craddock posed it, the problem was that preaching was too authoritarian.[5]

Craddock took a new look at how one preaches, arguing that to a "large extent [how one preaches] is *what* one preaches."[6] The problem as he saw it was that the theological *what* of a deductive method amounted to moralism and pedantry. He charged that the preacher imported concepts into the pulpit and delivered them to the congregation for their consumption. As he put it, the preacher "retails what he has somewhere, somehow obtained wholesale."[7] It is an essential part of the dynamic of this model that the congregation is put in the position of passively accepting whatever concepts the preacher foists on them. Regardless of whether the concepts themselves are authoritarian, the way they are presented, as a fait accompli, is itself authoritarian. And, according to Craddock, congregations resist "that movement of thought which asks at the outset the acceptance of a conclusion which the minister reached privately in his study or received by some special revelation."[8]

The turn toward induction that began over twenty years ago with the publication of *As One without Authority* is worth affirming today. It continues to receive a sympathetic hearing from those who have endured the dryness of unduly abstract preaching. Its foundation in the particular rings true to the dense, dynamic, and complex textures of life as it is actually lived. The swing of the pendulum away from a conceptual method is in many ways to be embraced. However, as with many reform movements, it has led some to go too far. It is possible, in an effort to avoid authoritarianism, to relinquish all authority. It is possible to focus so thoroughly on the *way* a sermon says something as to pay no heed to *what* is being said. It is possible to embrace the particular so thoroughly as to be unable to make any claims to the universal. Indeed, such extremes are not merely possible; far too frequently they are realities in the pulpits of North American Christian churches.

Craddock's educated hunch that preaching had become too

5. Craddock speaks of the "authoritarian foundation of traditional preaching" in the context of an important discussion of the deductive movement in preaching (*As One without Authority*, pp. 54ff.). He complains that "there is no democracy here, no dialogue, no listening by the speaker, no contributing by the hearer. If the congregation is on the team, it is as javelin catcher" (p. 55).

6. Craddock, *As One without Authority*, p. 52.

7. Craddock, *As One without Authority*, p. 43.

8. Craddock, *As One without Authority*, p. 125.

authoritarian was accurate twenty years ago, but it stands in need of some revision today. It is my educated hunch that the greatest threat to preaching today is not the authoritarian and moralistic sermon but the impenetrably particularized sermon that offers a scarcely discernible point.

Craddock and others provided an important corrective by steering us away from the reductionist tendency to pay too little attention to the form of a biblical text in a rush to the point, but the corrective can also be taken too far.[9] Indeed, something is lost when preaching is reduced to a single point — although it is not to say that in such cases preaching is pointless.[10] There should be a point to a sermon. A given biblical text will have a point, and a preacher preparing a sermon on that biblical text will need to make some decisions about the point of both the text and the sermon.[11]

Legitimate concern over biblical reductionism has had the unfortunate consequence of impugning the reputation of *concepts* in homiletic circles. The advantages of an inductive method are lost if an aversion to deductive logic devolves into an abandonment of all logic. Inductive preaching does not lack concepts; it simply reorients the direction of the movement to concepts. Rather than beginning with concepts and moving to particular-

---

9. Gail O'Day has suggested that "we need to ask ourselves if we move too quickly away from the text itself, from what the narrative does, how the story flows, and focus instead on some outline of events, some central point, on what the text is 'about'" (*The Word Disclosed: John's Story and Narrative Preaching* [St. Louis: CBP Press, 1987], p. 12).

10. Nor is it to suggest that Craddock advocates sermons without a point. It is simply the case that subsequent interpretation and development of Craddock's thesis has produced this unfortunate result. Craddock himself explicitly makes the case for sermons having a point: "Sermons that move inductively sustaining interest and engaging the listener do not have points any more than a narrative, a story, a parable, or even a joke has points. But there is a point, and the discipline of this one idea is creative in preparation, in delivery, and in reception of the message" (*As One without Authority*, p. 100).

11. David Buttrick has argued that the word *point* is not appropriate for describing preaching. He prefers the word *move*. "In speaking of 'moves,'" he says, "we are deliberately changing terminology. For years, preachers have talked of making points in sermons. The word 'point' is peculiar; it implies a rational, at-a-distance pointing at things, some kind of objectification" (*Homiletic: Moves and Structures* [Philadelphia: Fortress Press, 1987], p. 23). I wholly approve of the shift in emphasis signaled by the change in terminology from *point* to *move*. In using the word *move*, Buttrick is intentionally directing our focus to the dynamic character of preaching and arguing that the gospel ought not to be reduced to a neat system of points. But this is not really the issue here. I am here using the word *point* in the broader sense of a justification for preaching or a reason for preaching. I believe that preachers will have to make some decision about the point of it all if they are going to have anything worth saying.

ity, one moves from the particular to a concept. Preaching involves making up one's mind about a text and about a sermon, and this in turn involves a process of conceptualization. Without concepts it is not possible to transport what is true in one situation to another situation. If preaching is to have something to say, if it is to make real claims and exercise a legitimate authority, the whole notion of concepts will need to be rehabilitated.

Of course, rehabilitating concepts in the current context is no easy task. As Richard Eslinger observes, the "old topical/conceptual approach to preaching is critically, if not terminally ill."[12] His observation reflects a widely held dissatisfaction with concepts in preaching. The principal reason for the dissatisfaction is that, as Eslinger notes, "the old conceptual preaching simply is not heard by most of those in attendance."[13] The notion of concepts cannot be rehabilitated by a simple return to what Eslinger terms the "old conceptual method"; we will have to traverse carefully a course to a new place for concepts in preaching.

Concepts Gone Awry: The Case of the Biblical Theology Movement

It is surely more than coincidental that the criticism of a "conceptual method" in preaching parallels many of the criticisms of what has been called the biblical theology movement. Begun in the mid 1940s, the biblical theology movement had a tremendous impact on preaching in North America.[14] It eschewed topical preaching and strongly urged the exposition of biblical texts. As a movement, one of its chief aims was to reach beyond the "wasteland" of analytic biblical exegesis to a place where theological affirmations could be made. Making theological affirmations founded on biblical texts was grounded in the hermeneutical conviction that abiding concepts could be discerned in the Bible and could profitably be applied to the present.

The biblical theology movement had a great interest in biblical concepts. Its proponents often argued that rich and unique theological

12. Eslinger, *A New Hearing: Living Options in Homiletic Method* (Nashville: Abingdon Press, 1987), p. 11.

13. Eslinger, *A New Hearing*, p. 11.

14. For a history of the biblical theology movement, see Brevard S. Childs, *Biblical Theology in Crisis* (Philadelphia: Westminster Press, 1970).

concepts were buried in the words of Scripture.[15] For the preacher this proved a hermeneutical tour de force. The great chasm between the world of the Bible and the contemporary world could be bridged by a concept. The preacher as exegete could mine the words of a pericope for a preachable concept. Once found, the concept became a sermonic theme. The task of preaching such a concept was centered in finding the contemporary illustrative material to make the concept accessible and then convincing the congregation of its truth.

As a form of biblical scholarship and as a model for preaching, the biblical theology movement failed. In biblical scholarship it received a devastating blow with the publication of James Barr's *Semantics of Biblical Language* in 1961. Although further criticisms followed, it was Barr who shook its foundations.[16] He argued that the notion of uniquely biblical concepts latent in the words of Scripture stemmed from inappropriate and naive assumptions about semantics and the structure of language. Words cannot intelligibly be isolated from their contexts. The mere appearance of a particular word in a given pericope is no guarantee that it brings with it a theological richness. Words — even biblical words — are not direct and unambiguous markers of concepts.

For the preacher trained in the methods of the biblical theology movement, exegesis became excavation, digging through the riches of the past for a gem to be passed on to the present.[17] The Word of God was frequently equated with some Greek or Hebrew word. In fact, the biblical theology movement often made appeals to a unique Hebrew mind as part of an effort to identify a distinctive biblical perspective.[18] The claim was that the words of the Bible reflected, or gave expression to, this distinctive biblical perspective, which was additionally presumed to be superior to all other perspectives. The exegetical task, then, was to track down the particular concept of the biblical perspective coming to expression in a given word.

15. The translation of Gerhard Kittel's *Theologisches Wörterbuch zum neuen Testament* is the most significant monument to this aspect of the biblical theology movement.

16. "In reflecting on the effect of Barr's book, one cannot help being impressed with the success of his attack," says Brevard Childs. "Seldom has one book brought down so much superstructure with such effectiveness" (*Biblical Theology in Crisis*, p. 72).

17. A key tool for such exegetical excavation was etymology, the study of word origins and roots. A whole generation of congregations has been schooled on the differences between *chronos* and *kairos*, faith and truth, *dabar* and *logos*. For a splendid critique of etymological exegesis, see James Barr's discussion of the "root fallacy" in *The Semantics of Biblical Language* (Oxford: Oxford University Press, 1961), pp. 160-65.

18. On the connection between the "Hebrew mentality" and a "distinct biblical perspective," see Childs, *Biblical Theology in Crisis*, pp. 44-47.

When the proponents of the biblical theology movement felt they had located uniquely biblical concepts in the words of the Bible, they abstracted the concepts out of the context. In such a scheme, *what* a text says is important, not *how* it says it: content takes priority over form. In recent years, homiletics books have endorsed taking cues for biblical preaching from the Bible itself rather than taking the step of reducing biblical forms to biblical concepts. Scholars such as Amos Wilder have led many homileticians to give renewed attention to the inseparability of form and content in biblical texts and preaching.[19] Rushing to the central point, prematurely grasping what the text is about, separating what a text says from the way it says it — these are all mistakes commonly associated with the biblical theology movement.

The primary error of the biblical theology movement, however, lay in its presumption that behind the words or texts of Scripture were concepts. The specific failing lay not in the search for concepts as such but in the more fundamental presumption that concepts lay behind what was said.[20] What a text says is not some abstract entity existing on its own; it is always a matter of what the text says to a particular someone reading it. When our focus on a text shifts in this fashion, we see that the concept is not in the text, and certainly not behind the text, but rather is formed in the reading of the text, in the interaction between reader and text. This is not to downplay the role of the text in the formation of a concept; it is simply to say that the text itself contains no independent concept. When a reader forms a concept from a text, it is not the text's concept but the reader's concept, formed in the reading of the text.[21]

When the biblical theology movement spoke of biblical concepts, it

19. Wilder has stated that the "study of the rhetorical forms of the New Testament is not a superficial matter. Form and content cannot be long held apart. . . . The character of the early Christian speech-forms should have much to say to us with regard to our understanding of Christianity and its communication today" (*The Language of the Gospel: Early Christian Rhetoric* [New York: Harper & Row, 1964], pp. 12-13).

20. Such a search for concepts behind the texts of Scripture was merely another version of the "authorial intent fallacy" common to the Romantic hermeneutic. For a criticism of the authorial intent fallacy, see Richard Palmer, *Hermeneutics* (Evanston, Ill.: Northwestern University Press, 1969).

21. An excellent account of the process of reading a text can be found in Thomas G. Long's *Preaching and the Literary Forms of the Bible* (Philadelphia: Fortress Press, 1989); see especially pp. 11-22. In many ways, the genius of Craddock's *As One without Authority* resides in its attention to the dynamics of both reading a biblical text and preaching a sermon.

was in fact speaking of its own theological concepts which it had imported into the Bible. But this does not mean that there are no biblical concepts. Although flawed, the biblical theology movement did offer a hermeneutical advantage for preaching. Its focus on clear concepts allowed it to bridge the gap between the divergent worlds of the Bible and the contemporary setting. The preacher who determined that the concept of grace was what a particular text was all about could preach a sermon expounding on grace. The concept was portable and could easily be preached and illustrated for the contemporary congregation. Without the clear concepts of the biblical theology movement, preachers are left with few tools to make the connection between a biblical text and a congregation.

Storytelling and Preaching

Some have attempted to fill the vacuum created by the collapse of the biblical theology movement with storytelling.[22] Storytelling appears to meet the demand for a more inductive mode of preaching. In addition, because narrative is such a common biblical form, storytelling would seem to be a naturally appropriate form for preaching. Finally, storytelling provides an integrative framework for interpreting contemporary experience. Despite the rapid and broadly favorable reception of storytelling as a mode of preaching, however, it is not without problems.[23] For one thing, preaching has to involve more than mere storytelling. It is true that stories can enrich preaching by offering concrete elements that make it possible for the congregation to see, to perceive, to feel. Stories can rescue preached theology from the realm of abstraction. But it is also true that stories are opaque; one can easily be caught up in the detailed textures of a story and fail to look beyond it. Moreover, the particularity of a story ties it to a unique setting. If a preacher tells a story about Melinda, for instance, there is a sense in which the story is true only of Melinda and no one else until

22. There is a long list of books on storytelling and preaching; among the most important are Edmund A. Steimle, Morris J. Niedenthal, and Charles L. Rice, *Preaching the Story* (Philadelphia: Fortress Press, 1980); and Eugene L. Lowry, *The Homiletic Plot* (Nashville: Abingdon Press, 1980).

23. For a critique of storytelling in preaching, see Richard Lischer, "The Limits of Story," *Interpretation* 38 (January 1984). For a more recent treatment, see William Willimon, "Preaching as Entertainment," *Christian Century* 107 (1990): 204-6.

some other element is injected to transcend the particularity. But probably the most serious problem with storytelling in preaching involves deciding which stories to tell. For this, concepts are necessary.

In commenting on the importance of stories for preaching, Edmund Steimle and his colleagues describe three overlapping stories in preaching: the Bible's story, the preacher's story, and the congregation's story.[24] They argue that each story relates to the other. As many proponents of storytelling in preaching have seen, a well-told story often leads to the telling of another story. Charles Rice, for instance, has keenly observed that when you are approached and asked to tell a story, it is often difficult to come up with one, whereas if you are standing in a hallway with a group of friends who are telling stories, a story will come to mind almost automatically. One story leads to another, and you can hardly wait to tell your own.[25]

In any given sequence of stories, it is not always easy to trace the connections between one and the next. What are we to make of it if an account of a fishing expedition is followed by a narrative description of an infant's first footsteps. We depend on a concept to provide the connecting link between stories.[26] Without concepts, it is simply not possible to make a hermeneutical move from one particularity to another; one is left with the most radical kind of solipsism. When we do find a connection between diverse particulars, however, it is a concept that has afforded the vision.

Thus sermons must be more than mere storytelling just as they must be more than mere conceptual discourse. Properly, they are a continual movement from story to concept, from concept to story. The crucial decision of which story to tell and when to tell it depends on the grasp of a concept. The story of an infant's first steps following the story of a fishing expedition would not be a non sequitur if the connecting concept were the patience needed for both endeavors. Either explicitly or implicitly, sermons need to make a conceptual link between the stories they tell. The fact that concepts have fallen out of favor in preaching is not the fault of concepts themselves but of the ways in which they have been misused. We need to rehabilitate the notion of concepts in preaching.

24. See Steimle, Rice, and Niedenthal, *Preaching the Story*.

25. Rice made the observation in classroom instruction at Drew University in 1979.

26. On the critical importance of connective logic in sermon design, see David Buttrick's discussion of conjoining moves in sermons in *Homiletic*, pp. 69-79.

Concepts and Interpretation

Concepts are integral to preaching because preaching is fundamentally a hermeneutical discipline: preaching involves interpretation, which might be defined as a movement from the density of a given situation or symbol to the clarity and singularity of a concept. Certainly movement toward a concept is an indispensable element of interpretation, though it is not the only element. Concepts are not only the goal of interpretation but also tools that facilitate the process of interpretation. Concepts are misused in preaching when they are separated from this hermeneutical function. When they become things in themselves rather than integral elements in the process of interpretation, they are emptied of any meaning and are appropriately dismissed as "mere abstractions." But again, the fact that they can be misused does not mean that they should be avoided.

In an essay entitled "The Status of *Vorstellung* in Hegel's *Philosophy of Religion*," Paul Ricoeur explores an approach to interpretation that recognizes the significance of concepts. He carefully follows the contours of Hegel's notion of *Vorstellung* in the *Phenomenology of Spirit* and the *Berlin Lectures*. His argument makes it possible to discern an appropriate place for concepts in preaching. The full details of Ricoeur's argument are too complex to restate here, but we can touch on its major elements.

Ricoeur has long affirmed the importance of concepts, placing himself at odds with "the opponents of conceptual thinking."

> There is no need to deny the concept in order to admit that symbols give rise to an endless exegesis. If no concept can exhaust the requirement of further thinking borne by symbols, this idea signifies only that no given categorization can embrace all the semantic possibilities of a symbol. But it is the work of the concept alone that can testify to this surplus of meaning.[27]

Ricoeur examines Hegel's use of *Vorstellung* as a way of unfolding an approach to interpretation that can include conceptualization. *Vorstellung* can be translated in several different ways — as "representation," "idea," or, as Ricoeur prefers, "figurative thought." In Hegel's work, *Vorstellung* encompasses stories, symbols, and images. It might be called "picture-thinking," the sort of thinking one does in recalling the events of a

---

27. Ricoeur, *Interpretation Theory: Discourse and the Surplus of Meaning* (Fort Worth: Texas Christian University Press, 1976), p. 57.

day, recreating a picture of the events in one's mind, or in following a story by forming pictures in one's mind in an effort to piece together the elements of the account.[28]

Following Hegel, Ricoeur suggests that the process of interpretation connects "three components: immediacy, figurative mediation, and conceptualization."[29] The first component in the chain, immediacy, arises from something like a "nonhermeneutical moment," which is to say that before there can be figurative thought, something must happen to stimulate it. In the example of recalling the events of a day, immediacy would refer to the events themselves, before they are taken up in thought, before they are "pictured" or figured in one's mind.

The phase of immediacy does not stand on its own. It passes over into figurative thought. In all but fleeting thoughts, figurative thought is formed in language, story, or symbol. Then figurative thought yields to "conceptualization," the concluding formation of a concept. It is only when one makes the full movement from immediacy through figurative thought to the formation of a concept that the "picture thought" yields a meaning.

By way of example, consider a beginning geometry student looking at several examples of right-angled parallelograms in the classroom. The phase of looking at the parallelograms is the phase of immediacy. This is something akin to a nonhermeneutical moment because the student has not yet formed a "picture" in her mind out of the lines on the page. Once she does form such a picture in her mind, interpretation has passed into the second phase, figurative mediation. At this point, the student has only interpreted the immediate perceptions of the examples of parallelograms into mental pictures of the individual rectangles she has observed. It is not until she links the common features of the various examples together and grasps the defining concept of the rectangle as a four-sided equal-angled plane figure that she attains the final phase of conceptualization. She then grasps a concept that transcends every particular instance.

The movement in the interpretative process that results in a concept follows what Ricoeur calls "the inner dynamism" of figurative thought. He tersely describes this conceptualization process as follows:

28. This process is similar to the one described by W. G. Gallie in *Philosophy and the Historical Understanding,* 2d ed. (New York: Schocken Books, 1968), pp. 22ff.

29. Ricoeur, "The Status of *Vorstellung* in Hegel's Philosophy of Religion," in *Meaning, Truth, and God,* ed. Leroy S. Rouner (Notre Dame, Ind.: University of Notre Dame Press, 1982), p. 87.

a) The dynamism of representation is secured by the thrust of figurative thought toward speculative thought.
b) The concept is the endless death of the representation.
c) The concept is nothing without the dying process of the representation: it is the ability to recapitulate thoughtfully the inner dynamism of the representation.[30]

In speaking of the "dynamism of representation," Ricoeur is referring to a presumption that interpreters bring to whatever they are seeking to interpret — namely, that there is something being said there. The dynamism resides in the movement from (1) the act or fact of "saying" (the entity of a text, a symbol, a story, a situation), to (2) the point that it says something, to (3) the point that we have a something "said." When we read a text, see a symbol, hear a story, or encounter a situation, we are not satisfied until we have some sense of what it means. We are not satisfied with a "saying" in itself; we seek to discern what it means — that is, to come to the "said." This seeking to know what it means is what Ricoeur means when he speaks of the "thrust from figurative thought to speculative thought."

The movement from the "saying" to what is "said" takes place in and through the "saying," which is to say that we can't have a concept, a "said," without a "saying."[31] But, of the two, the concept is usually considered to be the more important. If Jim engages Jane in conversation, he expresses himself audibly. The collection of words, phrases, sentences, and inflections that he produces constitutes the "saying," and although it is important that Jane literally hear what Jim says in order to understand him, it is not nearly as important, either to Jim or to Jane, as is Jane's grasping what it is that Jim means when he says what he says.

When Ricoeur speaks of the "death of the representation," he means that once the "saying" serves its function, it passes away. Once Jane has comprehended what Jim "said," Jim's actual spoken words are no longer important, and they pass from the scene. Having gotten us to the "said," the "saying" becomes irrelevant.

30. Ricoeur, "The Status of *Vorstellung* in Hegel's Philosophy of Religion," p. 87.
31. In this regard, Ricoeur and Craddock are agreed that the movement of thought is from particular to universal. On the inductive aspects in Ricoeur's thought, see his description of the relationship between words and sentences in "Structure, Word, Event," in *The Conflict of Interpretations,* ed. Don Ihde (Evanston, Ill.: Northwestern University Press, 1974), pp. 79-96.

Ricoeur views interpretation as a dynamic process that moves from the density of the particular instance (i.e., a symbol, a situation, or an event) to the transparency of thought. It involves moving from immediacy through figurative thought to a concept or speculative thought. But he also contends that interpretation cannot end in speculative thought. If a concept fails to return to the density of a symbol, situation, or event, it is emptied of its content. This is what Ricoeur means when he says that the concept involves the endless death of the representation. In order to grasp the concept, we must transcend the opacity of the particular. The figurative thought must die to itself to yield the concept. But this dying must be endless. What is said in a representation, a figurative thought, cannot survive on its own: it must return to representation, story, symbol. On its own, the "said" is not a "said" at all but something waiting to be said. This is why it is possible to speak of "mere" concepts: without the moment of representation, they are empty, vacuous.

Returning to the example of the geometry student, we might say that the concept of the rectangle is empty until it is taken up in a particular instance. Abstracted from the examples in the classroom, the concept is an empty definition. The student who knows that a rectangle is a right-angled parallelogram has only the half of the concept rectangle. It is not until the student looks at a door or piece of typing paper and recognizes that its parallel sides and right angles constitute the borders of a rectangle that the concept returns from abstraction and takes on a new figurative mediation.

Ricoeur contends that religious hermeneutics involves just such a circular process. The hermeneutical process

1. keeps starting from and returning to the moment of religious immediacy (variously known as a religious experience, a Word-Event, or a kerygmatic moment);
2. keeps generating stories, symbols, and associated interpretations in the midst of a confessing and interpreting community; and
3. keeps aiming at conceptual thought without severing its roots in the initial immediacy of religion or in the mediating shapes of figurative thought.[32]

32. See Ricoeur, "The Status of *Vorstellung* in Hegel's Philosophy of Religion," pp. 78-88.

The circularity of a religious hermeneutics means that it is never enough to have any one aspect of religious discourse in isolation. Founding religious events cannot be isolated from their appropriation by the communities that tell and retell their story. By the same token, the telling in story and symbol cannot be isolated from the appropriation of their meaning in conceptual thought. And conceptual thought cannot be isolated from its return to further telling or retelling of its stories and symbols. These new stories and symbols, however, must again make the movement from figurative thought toward concepts and thus come full circle once again.

Concepts in Preaching

Applied to biblical preaching, the circularity of a religious hermeneutics looks like this:

1. Coming out of a congregation, the preacher reads a biblical text and forms a figurative mediation, a "picture-thought."[33]
2. Following the inner dynamism of the figurative mediation, the preacher comes to a concept.
3. Having grasped the concept, the preacher returns it to a new figurative mediation.
4. This new figurative mediation forms the core image or story system in the sermon.
5. The preacher uses this image or story system to help the congregation grasp the concept shared between the biblical text and the sermon.
6. The congregation forms a figurative mediation, a "picture thought" from the sermon.
7. Following the inner dynamism of their figurative mediation from the sermon, the congregation grasps a concept.
8. Aided by the sermon, the congregation begins to form their own figurative mediations from the concept shared between biblical text, the sermon, and now themselves.

33. For a thorough description of the preacher coming out of the congregation, see Thomas G. Long, *The Witness of Preaching* (Louisville: Westminster/John Knox, 1989), pp. 9-13.

9. The circle is completed when the congregation's figurative mediations are shared by the preacher, who again returns to a biblical text.

Thus the task of biblical exegesis clearly rests on the presumption that the text has something to say. We are not satisfied with just reading the text; we want to know what it means. And in order to come to the meaning of the text, we have to follow its inner dynamism. In this context, form and content are indeed inseparable. We have to pay attention to *how* a text says what it says — although it is also the case that the *how* is not our principal focus of interest: we are more interested in *what* it says than how it says it. The point of discerning what the text says is a matter of coming to a concept, a thought that is no longer simply a picture of what is described or narrated in the text but a thought set free from the mediating element of the text itself, free from this particularity, and consequently open to a new particularity. Having once arrived at this point, however, the concept must return to some new particularity. It cannot retain meaning on its own; it has to be connected to a new representation, a new figurative mediation. If a text says something, it must say what it says again in a new context, or it says nothing at all.

It is, of course, possible for a text to say what it says again in the self-same mediation from which it has just spoken — that is to say, the text can be repeated verbatim — but that is not preaching. Genuine preaching involves finding a new mediation, a new way of saying what is said in a biblical text. Exegesis of a biblical text leads to a concept. Having arrived at this point, the preacher must not stop the process and simply present and illustrate this concept. That is what happened in what Richard Eslinger calls the "old conceptual method." There is no doubt that this can be done, and Eslinger may well be right in asserting that many pastors persist in doing it.[34] The problem is that in presenting and illustrating the concept the preacher fails to take the hermeneutical process full circle. A concept that does not take on a new figurative mediation may say what the text is *saying*, but it does not say what the text *says* — that is, it may

---

34. Eslinger describes the situation this way: "Preachers gather in workshops on their craft and chuckle when the leader refers to 'three points and a poem.' Yet many pastors return from such events and continue to preach the propositions and illustrations mainly because for them 'it's always been done this way,' and it has become a familiar and seemingly harmless habit" (*A New Hearing*, p. 11).

manage to present the point of the text, but only in a disinterested way. In such a presentation, it doesn't matter whether the concept is true or false, interesting or tedious. To say what a text *says* — to preach genuinely — the preacher has to go beyond mere presentation and illustration and return the concept to figurative thought. To do this, the preacher will need to draw on some figurative mediation — a story perhaps, or at the very least an image or symbol. Then the concepts of the text can become the concepts of the sermon; what the text says can become what the sermon says.

The preacher undertakes this hermeneutical procedure out of a conviction that the Bible has something to say that needs to be said. But the preacher remains aware of the fact that the task of preaching is not simply to tell a congregation what the Bible says but to *say* the same thing the Bible says.[35] Just as the preacher comes to the text with the expectation that there is something here to be said, the congregation comes to the sermon with the expectation that there is something to be said. The congregation follows the sermon as a figurative mediation that yields a concept. The congregation must also turn the concept to a figurative mediation. Again, this may be done by using the self-same figurative mediation of the sermon.[36] But such a restatement of the sermon is not enough. It is akin to the rote memorization that a student demonstrates at the beginning of the learning process. The real "Aha!" comes not when the student remembers the definition of a rectangle but when the concept of the rectangle finds a particular instance of the student's own making. The congregation's ability to put a concept in motion, to return it to figurative mediation, is the measure of the effectiveness of preaching.

35. This is what Karl Barth had in mind in making his distinction between illustration and interpretation: "Illustration is saying the same thing *in other words.* Interpretation is saying the *same thing* in other words."

36. One of the greatest strengths of David Buttrick's *Homiletic* is his insistence that the sermon form in consciousness. Buttrick tends to measure this forming in consciousness by a congregation's ability to remember what a preacher says. On this point, I think, Buttrick is only half right. If the congregation can remember what the preacher said, I will grant that they have conceptually grasped what the sermon says, but I would argue that this amounts to only a minimal forming in consciousness. If the concept is to belong to more than just the preacher, it will have to generate a new figurative mediation on the part of the listeners. And in this process, the movement of the sermon itself is a secondary matter: the preacher's figurative mediation can appropriately pass away once the concept is grasped and carried on.

Conclusion

Preaching is an interpretive activity. All interpretation involves conceptualization. Nevertheless, conceptualization constitutes just one moment in the process of interpretation. To come to a concept is to make the movement from the saying to the said. One "has" the said when one has a concept. But we have to move beyond this point. Conceptualization involves a continual dialectical movement from figurative thinking in the representation to speculative thinking beyond the representation and then back again to figurative thought.

Biblical preaching needs concepts to move beyond the opacity of biblical texts. And yet, as recent homileticians have established, sermons that merely reduce biblical texts to concepts are not biblically faithful. This is not because there are no concepts in the Bible. If there were no biblical concepts, the biblical texts would not be about anything, and preachers would have nothing to say. In order to have something to say, preachers have to decide what a text is about. At some point the text has to be interpreted, and the process of interpretation will necessarily involve coming to a concept. As Ricoeur says, texts are discourse, and discourse says something about something.[37] Until preachers decide what a text is about, they have nothing to say.

Although coming to a concept is an indispensable moment in the process of interpretation, it is not the last moment. Although the concept makes it possible to grasp what the text says in thought, coming to a concept falls short of saying what the text says. Preachers who do no more present concepts may enlighten their congregations, but they will not be able to transform them. Transformation will take place only when the congregation takes up the interpretive work themselves, when they speak the gospel in their own lives.[38]

Christian preaching brings to its task the presumption that there

---

37. Ricoeur, *Interpretation Theory,* p. 12.

38. Craddock has this sort of congregational participation in mind when he says, "Realistic and responsible biblical preaching means bearing the awesome burden of interpreting Scripture *for the congregation to which one preaches.* This does not mean that it is the preacher's responsibility to hand down a more or less authoritative interpretation for them, but as pastor-preacher he will lead them into the experience of hearing the message of Scripture for their situations. This calls for real courage, courage that moves ahead even while dreadfully conscious of the pitfalls of eisegesis and the thousand chances to be proven wrong by history" (*As One without Authority,* p. 128).

is something that needs to be said. If it does not presume this, then silence is the more prudent course. Congregations rightly expect preaching to say something. The ultimate measure of effective preaching is not just that the something said of the sermon is *heard* by the congregation but that the something said can and is *said* by the congregation.[39] When this happens, the Word again becomes flesh and dwells among us.

---

39. On the importance of the congregation saying the gospel, see Buttrick, *Homiletic*, pp. 225-34.

Toward a Hermeneutics of the Solo Savior: Dirty Harry and Romans 5–8

Bernard Brandon Scott

Rudolf Bultmann proclaimed a motto that inflamed his critics but is a truism. Theology, he said, is anthropology.[1] Perhaps in a graphic age this should be printed: *theo*logy is *anthropo*logy. While Bultmann had Paul's theology in mind, it would seem that any time one deals "with God not as he is in Himself but only with God as He is significant for man, for man's responsibility and man's salvation," then Bultmann's motto would be true.

Is the inverse likewise true? Is anthropology theology? If so, it means that even those statements about humanity that have no obvious referent to God betray inevitably a premise about God. Moreover, if the way in which we depict the world and humanity implicitly conjure up a depiction of God, then the ways in which movies depict humanity in the world will reflect assumptions about God, whether present or absent or even dead.

Mythical Structure

America's frontier experience, as Alexis de Tocqueville long ago pointed out, led to an accent on the individual and freedom of action for the

---

1. Bultmann, *Theology of the New Testament,* vol. 2 (New York: Scribner's, 1955), p. 191. Bultmann is speaking of Paul, but his position is very applicable to our situation.

individual unknown in old Europe.[2] But this accent on the individual has combined with our ideological commitment to capitalism to produce a new version of the hero myth in the form of the rugged individualist or solo savior.[3] The insidious nature of myth is that it functions without our knowing it, shaping our expectations about the world and hence the way we view it and behave in it. Further, we expect others, both modern and ancient, to behave according to the coordinates of our myths.[4]

The power of myth is such that unbeknownst to us we conform the image of other heroes to fit the pattern of our myth. A classic example is the standard image of the apostle Paul. Various scholars have protested for over a generation against the individualization of Paul.[5] There has been a tendency to view Paul as the lone individual, fighting against the Jerusalem group and standing up for the rights of the individual as symbolized in the slogan "By Faith Alone." Paul the missionary struggles alone in his missionary activity.

This individualized picture of Paul seriously distorts the historical record. Paul's self-understanding is corporate, and his emphasis is not on the individual or even individual conversion but on the community as the body of Christ or the people of God. In baptism and faith the individual is lost into the body of Christ, so "It is no longer I who live, but Christ who lives in me" (Gal. 2:20). Paul frequently refers to coworkers, and most of the letters have several addressees. Abetted by the image in Acts, we imagine Paul as a powerful speaker and preacher even though the Corinthians had a slogan that warns us otherwise — "His letters are weighty and strong, but his bodily presence is weak, and his speech of no account"

2. For an extended assessment of Tocqueville's insights into the American character in *Democracy in America,* see Robert N. Bellah, Richard Madsen, William M. Sullivan, Ann Swidler, and Steven M. Tipton, *Habits of the Heart: Individualism and Commitment in American Life* (Berkeley and Los Angeles: University of California Press, 1985).

3. This analysis belongs to a broader typology of the American hero that I am in the process of developing. The traditional hero who saves the community or world from threatened evil is perhaps best represented in the classic western *Shane.* Two distinct refinements of the traditional myth in the context of the American experience are the Horatio Alger hero and the John Wayne hero. Dirty Harry is a mutation of the Duke's characters, and it appears that Robocop is a further mutation of the Dirty Harry hero.

4. On the sense of myth employed here, see my *Hear Then the Parable* (Minneapolis: Fortress Press, 1989), pp. 37-39.

5. See, e.g., Krister Stendahl, "The Apostle Paul and the Introspective Conscience of the West," in *Paul among Jews and Gentiles and Other Essays* (Philadelphia: Fortress Press, 1976), pp. 78-96.

(2 Cor. 10:10). We go further and imagine Paul as constantly involved in preaching activity. Yet a recent work on Paul the tentmaker has reminded us that his occupation placed him among the scorned lower classes.[6] When he protests that "we worked night and day, so that we might not burden any of you" (1 Thess. 2:9), he is not exaggerating. The context of his ministry was neither the parish nor the boardroom nor the TV nor even the agora but the workshop.

The invasive power of myth allows it to operate in and shape our construction of reality without our being aware of it.[7] We inevitably, almost naturally, reconstruct and constrain the way we perceive reality so as to fit it into our readily available mythical structures. It takes effort, self-awareness, and self-criticism to stand back and examine our mythical heritage.

John Wayne: The Duke

The rugged individualist myth is not a constant. It has undergone development and elaboration as our culture and history have shifted. A classic incarnation of the rugged individualist was the cowboy, and the cauldron that produced the myth was Hollywood.

The John Wayne persona as developed in a number of famous westerns became the epitome of the myth. The nickname "Duke" conjures up this image. The Duke character is a lovable scoundrel. Wayne summarized the persona in his description of Rooster Cogburn: he has "been around long enough to know for sure that you don't mess with outlaws, but use every trick in book, fair or foul, to bring them to justice."[8] He is loyal to his family and those he loves. Though often on the periphery of society, he is never an outlaw, even though he frequently engages in semi-lawless activity. He believes that to bring about justice, the finery of justice at times has to be violated. Such behavior was justified mythically

6. Ronald F. Hock, *The Social Context of Paul's Ministry: Tentmaking and Apostleship* (Philadelphia: Fortress Press, 1980).

7. "Myths operate in men's minds without their being aware of the fact," wrote Claude Lévi-Strauss (*The Raw and the Cooked,* trans. John Weightman and Doreen Weightman [New York: Harper & Row, 1969], p. 12).

8. Wayne, quoted by Jon Tuska in *The Filming of the West* (Garden City, N.Y.: Doubleday, 1976), p. 576. Tuska outlines the importance of the Duke persona in the western mythology.

in a variety of ways. The expanding and almost limitless range of the frontier justified certain unusual behavior. The normal was reserved to the settled East, with its crowded spaces and established law. In the West's limitless and empty spaces, the individual had to be self-sufficient and resourceful. As one of the characters in *Shane* (1953) notes, there was no law in the valley. Individuals had to take the law into their own hands. The myth of the West also supported a strong belief in the integrity of the individual who can rise above the circumstances to triumph over the immediate. John Wayne's westerns, like almost all westerns, were nostalgic. They looked back to the past as a way of providing a guiding light in the present. It was indeed a powerful mythos.

The Duke in the City

In a series of movies built around the character Inspector Harry Callahan, Clint Eastwood has explored the Duke myth in an urban American context.[9] Translating this myth into this context has proven somewhat problematic. The significant impression that these movies have made on America's language and memory indicates that they have hit on a theme of importance, however, a point of conflict between reality and myth in the nation's life.[10] The conflict that these movies attempt to resolve is easy to spot: the perceived breakdown of civilized values in urban American life. This conflict is frequently projected onto a legal system that ostensibly protects the "rights" of the criminal at the expense of the "rights" of the victim or law-abiding citizen. But while the Dirty Harry movies were produced in the wake of the Miranda decision, they cannot be fully accounted for in terms of a reaction to that new emphasis in the law. The

9. Toward the end of his career, Wayne characterized Clint Eastwood as "my only logical successor" (quoted by Boris Vnijewski in *The Films of Clint Eastwood* [Secaucus, N.J.: Citadel Press, 1983], p. 10). Both Wayne and Eastwood were the most popular male box office attractions of their generation. Eastwood's first real success was in the TV series *Rawhide*, which was inspired by the classic Howard Hawks western *Red River* (1948), starring John Wayne.

10. See Jim Miller, "Clint Eastwood: A Different Kind of Western Hero," in *Shooting Stars: Heroes and Heroines of Western Film*, ed. Archie P. McDonald (Bloomington, Ind.: Indiana University Press, 1987), pp. 189-90. This issue has also been taken up in the area of social sciences; see, e.g., Carl B. Klochars, "The Dirty Harry Problem," *Annals of the American Academy of Political and Social Science* (1980): 33-47.

conflict goes deeper; the films expose a profound ambiguity in American life — on the one hand our perception of ourselves as peace-loving, the new Israel, the blessed nation, and on the other hand our history of violence in defense of that peace.

Some of these themes are part of the western myth as represented by the Duke. The West was frequently portrayed as a place in which law had to be established by methods that were sometimes lawless. Yet in the Dirty Harry movies, the city is a place of terror where the law is frequently interpreted in such a way as to turn against those who are lawful. The threat and terror are much more ominous than in traditional westerns. The world of the traditional western is forward-looking, anticipating salvation (eschatological). The world of Dirty Harry is corrupt and fallen, beyond hope of salvation. In the western, God is present as future promise. In the Dirty Harry movies, God is absent; there is no foreseeable end to the evil, and only the lone individual can even survive the system much less triumph over it.

This shift from a West of wide-open spaces to a western city creates conflict for the hero. To the extent that Harry Callahan is the embodiment of the Duke's values in the new city, he is a throwback, an anachronism. Indeed, others frequently refer to Harry as a dinosaur, outdated, a product of a bygone age. He does not belong to the modern urban period. Some critics have condemned the movies as reactionary and fascist.[11]

The Dirty Harry Cycle

A double conflict drives the mythical structure of the Dirty Harry movies. The world (the city) is evil, irredeemably so. Theologically, this constitutes a striking parallel to the view of the ancient Manichaeans. Not only do the Manichaeans and Dirty Harry share a dualist view of the world, but both likewise advocate a kind of asceticism as a solution to the problem. While Callahan is not religious as such, he is a type of ascetic. He forms few human relationships — he has neither family nor wife, cannot keep a partner, and is isolated within the police department. Unlike the James

11. Pauline Kael, e.g., refers to the Dirty Harry movie as a right-wing fantasy (*5001 Nights at the Movies* [New York: Holt, Rinehart & Winston, 1984], p. 148).

Bond hero, he is not addicted to technological marvels.[12] He is an urban ascetic. But the question remains why his world is irredeemably evil.

The second conflict in the Dirty Harry mythology derives from the attempt to translate the values of Duke into the city. This sets Harry's values at odds with those of the modern world. In one sense, westerns also faced this problem: their values were nostalgic from the point of view of the contemporary viewer and filmmaker. But in another sense, their values were not anachronistic within the setting of the action they presented. They had the romantic luxury of being able to look forward to a new future in which all would be right and we could return to the mythical equivalent of the Garden of Eden. To put it more prosaically, the hero of the western could ride off into a sunset that predated our dawn. But Dirty Harry movies don't have that romantic option; they present a conflict of values that is real, felt, and unresolved. At the end of a Dirty Harry movie, there is no hope of a Garden of Eden, an eschatological solution. They are a series of stories caught in a conflict between the values of Duke and the values of the modern city. Each of the five similarly structured movies advances a different problem in contemporary morals.

The Mythical Setting Scene

All of the movies open with a set sequence that establishes the tone of the film. The hero, Inspector Callahan, is never shown in these opening shots. *Dirty Harry* (1971) opens with a high shot of a girl swimming in a penthouse pool. The view is urban, skyscrapers all around. The camera swoops in on another rooftop and sights down the barrel of a rifle. The rifle fires, and the girl floats dead in the pool. In the next scene, the penthouse is crawling with police going about their various tasks. Callahan appears, alone, separate from the rest. He walks around and then goes by himself to the adjoining rooftop and finds the spent cartridge.

This initial scene defines the world and the protagonist. The world is urban, ominous, dangerous, violent without warning. The high point of view taken by the camera does not signify transcendence but evil. It is not some god overlooking the horizon but evil lurking on the rooftop. Callahan

---

12. The James Bond movies are more clearly meant to be viewed as a kind of fantasy, whereas the Dirty Harry movies are set more in the mode of gritty realism.

is defined by silence and isolation from the other police. He has no partner. Physically, he is tall, lean, hard-boiled, a man of few words — the archetypical cowboy in a suit. There is a strong intertextual referent deriving from the fact that most of Eastwood's earlier career was in westerns.

Early on in each of the movies, Callahan faces a test that establishes his derring-do. All take place while Harry is eating, normally an act of bonding or socializing with other people. In *Dirty Harry*, he is eating a hot dog at a luncheonette when he spots over his shoulder a car parked in front of a bank. He coolly waits for the action to begin while telling the short-order cook to phone the police. "Now if they'll just wait until the cavalry arrives." But of course that is not going to happen; it never happens in Dirty Harry's world. The robbers run out of the bank and Harry takes off after them, a .44 Magnum in one hand, hot dog in the other. He shoots the robbers down one by one, creating mayhem in the street. Finally, he walks up to one wounded robber who is reaching for a sawed-off shotgun. Standing over him, sighting down the long barrel of his pistol, Callahan says, "I know what you're thinking, punk. You're thinking, 'Did he fire five shots or six?' Well, to tell the truth, in all this confusion I forgot myself. But being as this is a .44 magnum, and the most powerful handgun in the world — it can clean blow your head off — you've got to ask yourself one question: 'Do I feel lucky?' Well, do you punk?" As the man withdraws his hand from the shotgun, Harry turns and walks away. Then the robber calls after him: "I gotta know." Harry turns, points the gun at him, and pulls the trigger. The gun is empty.

These formula scenes recurring in each movie set the mythical landscape for the hero. It is a type of western shoot-out on concrete and asphalt instead of a dirt street lined with wooden storefronts. The urban crowdedness underscores the sense of evil claiming innocent bystanders at random. Callahan, with his weapon as his partner, always plays the traditional gunfighter role in such situations. The audience often views these scenes through the gun sight, or, failing that, we are made aware of the presence of Callahan's weapon. In *The Enforcer* (1976), after Callahan has rescued a group taken hostage during a robbery by driving a car through the window of the building in which they are being held and methodically shooting the robber-terrorists, his captain charges him with having put on a wild West show. In *Magnum Force* (1973) he interrupts a meal at an airport restaurant to come to the rescue of a hijacked airplane. In *Sudden Impact* (1983) he takes on a group of men robbing a diner at which he regularly eats. Obviously outnumbered, he tells them to put down their guns "because *we*'re just not going to let you walk out of here." When one of them asks "Who's 'we'?" he replies "Smith and Wesson." The gun is all Callahan needs in his contest against the larger foe. In *The Dead Pool* (1988) the scene is a Chinese restaurant. Callahan and his partner are outside when suddenly an explosion sends a man sailing through the front window. Callahan sends his partner to call for backup while he goes to the rescue. Inside the restaurant, several robbers are terrorizing the clients. Callahan enters and sneaks into a booth. One of the robbers trains a gun on him. Callahan hands him the fortune from a fortune cookie: "It says you're shit out of luck." He draws his gun and starts blowing away the bad guys. One of them escapes into the street, where he is subdued by Callahan's partner.

In these scenes, all of which are basically unrelated to the movies' plots, the action serves to underscore the point that the cavalry never shows up, that Callahan must always stand alone. The only variation on the theme comes in *The Dead Pool,* and in that case, Callahan's partner does not so much come to the rescue as join in the fray.[13]

A Monster Set Free: *Dirty Harry*

The plot of *Dirty Harry* revolves around the pursuit of a vicious killer calling himself Scorpio. But this is not a simple chase movie in which the object is to catch the killer before he kills again. The movie's subtext paints the breakdown of a society. Callahan and Scorpio (Anthony Robinson) are as much symbols for values as they are characters in the story.

Scorpio sends a note to the mayor of San Francisco in which he explains that he had kidnaped a fourteen-year-old girl and buried her alive; he will let her die unless he gets $100,000. The mayor agrees to pay the ransom over Callahan's protests that the girl is already dead and they should not pay. Callahan is chosen to deliver the ransom, and against orders he takes his partner along. After leading Callahan from phone to phone on a tense chase around the city, Scorpio brutally attacks him at the foot of a towering cross in a park. "I've changed my mind," he shouts. "I'm going

13. *The Dead Pool* introduces a number of other exceptions to the normal pattern of Dirty Harry movies as well. This may simply be an indication that the series has run out of steam.

to let her die." Callahan's partner attempts to come to his aid but is shot by Scorpio. The wounded Callahan stabs Scorpio in the leg with a knife he had strapped to his ankle, but the injured kidnaper manages to escape nonetheless. Callahan passes out at the foot of the cross. The brutality of this scene is characteristic of many climactic scenes in the Dirty Harry movies. Although the symbolism of the cross is blatant, the sacrificial slaughter saves no one. All escape bleeding and wounded. It's a kind of madness that ends nothing, stands for nothing.

Callahan traces Scorpio to his hiding place in a large stadium and shoots him in his good leg. Scorpio immediately demands his right to see a lawyer. Callahan stands over him with his .44 Magnum and demands to know where he has buried the girl. The scene dissolves with the implication that Callahan will get the information he wants. In the next scene, we see a nude girl's body being removed from a shallow grave in the early morning mist.

If this were a mere chase movie, it would have climaxed with Callahan's capture of Scorpio. But the narrative object of this film is not Scorpio's capture.

The district attorney releases Scorpio on the grounds that Callahan had violated his civil rights. The law declares Scorpio the innocent victim and Callahan the criminal, leading Callahan to say, "Well, the law is crazy." This scene stakes out a double point of view: Callahan's and the law's. Callahan represents the values of the Duke (sometimes you have to bend the law in order to bring about real justice), whereas the district attorney represents the law. From Callahan's perspective he is the hero — doing his job, bringing the slime of the earth to justice. From the district attorney's perspective, Scorpio is innocent until proven guilty, and Callahan has engaged in criminal behavior by violating his rights. The Duke faced crooked law enforcement officers, but Callahan has to face the law itself as enemy.

Scorpio responds by pursuing a vendetta against Callahan. He pays to have himself horribly beaten and then charges Callahan with having inflicted the wounds, claiming police brutality. When confronted, Callahan remarks, "Anyone can see I didn't do it 'cause he looks too damn good."

The plot now pushes toward its climax. Scorpio kidnaps a group of children in a school bus and demands money and a plane to take him out of the country. The mayor agrees. Callahan doesn't. "When are you guys going to quit fooling around with this man?" He finally catches up with Scorpio, who holds a child hostage and demands that Harry throw down his gun. Callahan feigns compliance but then shoots. Dazed and bleeding, Scorpio reaches for his gun, which gives Callahan the opportunity to repeat the movie's opening scene. "In the excitement I plumb forgot how many times I fired. Do you feel lucky?" Scorpio goes for his gun and Harry shoots him dead. The focus shifts to Harry, who removes his badge and throws it away. The camera pulls back to a high vantage point, like an omniscient narrator. But again it is not a God's-eye view; it is a portrait of a world of loss — a gravel pit, the dregs of a culture. Callahan has abandoned the law.

The Partner

Throughout all five Dirty Harry movies much is made of the dangers of being Callahan's partner. As he himself remarks, "They usually end up dead." Misfortune does uniformly befall his partners. The movies always begin and end with him working alone. But while they survive, the partners do serve as useful foils for the Dirty Harry character.

In *Dirty Harry* the partner, Gonzales (Remi Santoni), is a college graduate with a degree in sociology. Gonzales is typical of Callahan's partners. They come from minority groups, appear to be better educated, and represent urban values in contrast with Harry's Duke values. In *Magnum Force* the partner is a black, in *The Enforcer* a woman, and in *The Dead Pool* an Oriental. Needless to say, Callahan isn't easy to get along with. On first meeting Gonzales he says, "Don't let your college degree get you killed." Yet inevitably there is a bonding between Callahan and his partner, and each develops a grudging respect for the other. In several cases, the partners even manage to modify Callahan's worldview.

The partners serve as bridges or mediators between Callahan and the world he believes has betrayed him. The bonding between Callahan and Gonzales reaches its high point when Callahan violates orders and takes him along on the ransom drop. The bonding between Callahan and his partner frequently involves some violation of the law, some instance in which the partner steps over the line to join Harry. Gonzales serves the plot by providing a backup for Callahan, but, more important for the film's message, he is an educated man who proves willing to respond to the system by disobeying orders, who is willing to become lawless and dirty like Harry. After Gonzales is seriously wounded, Callahan visits him in the hospital, and Gonzales tells him that he will not be returning to the force. His wife says that it is her fault, that she just cannot take it. When she innocently asks how Callahan's wife takes it, he replies that she was killed by a drunk. "Why do you stay in?" she asks. "I don't know," he replies. "I really don't."

Callahan ends as he began — alone, alienated from a world he is trying to save. Even more, he is a hero who does not know why he continues his quest.

What's Dirty about Harry?

In the series' first movie, the question of how Callahan got the nickname "Dirty Harry" comes up several times. The captain offers the first explanation when he explains that Harry hates everybody (at which point Callahan provides an object lesson by spitting out a list of derogatory names for ethnic groups). The second explanation is provided by Gonzales when he catches Harry watching a couple making love: Harry is dirty because he is a voyeur.[14] A third explanation of Harry's nickname crops up after he has been assigned to deliver the ransom demanded by Scorpio. "No wonder they call him Dirty Harry," one of the characters remarks. "He always gets the shit job." While there are a variety of explanations for the appellation *Dirty*, in the end they all boil down to the same thing: Harry is unclean, a scapegoat, a man whose violence protects and purifies the society that rejects both him and his values.

The Innocent Killers — *Magnum Force*

The moral calculus of *Magnum Force* is very different from that of *Dirty Harry.* In *Dirty Harry,* Callahan himself appears at times to be a vigilante,

---

14. The theme of voyeurism runs throughout the movie. In one scene, Harry is on a stakeout and trains his binoculars on an attractive naked woman in an apartment across the way. (He later finds out that she is a lesbian and is disgusted.) Publicity materials for the Dirty Harry films often feature a stone-faced Callahan hiding behind a pair of impenetrable sunglasses, looking out at an alien and, to his tastes, disgusting world. And of course the movie camera implicates the viewer in the voyeurism as well: we see what Harry sees when he looks through his sunglasses and his binoculars.

but in *Magnum Force* he faces off against a squad of vigilantes within the San Francisco Police Force. Vigilante justice was a theme of many westerns; in *Magnum Force* the vigilantes ride motorcycles instead of horses.

During the movie's opening credits, the camera focuses on a .44 Magnum, Callahan's gun, providing one clear sense of the movie's title. In the first scene, a man, presumably an organized crime figure, leaves a courthouse after having been freed from murder charges on a technicality. He gets into a waiting limousine and pulls away from a hostile crowd. A motorcycle cop follows the car and then signals for the driver to pull over. The officer, whose face we never see, pulls his gun and shoots all the passengers in the limousine. The juxtaposition of the .44 Magnum of the credits and the execution of the four men in the car sets up the movie's moral calculus. What constitutes legitimate violence?

The death squad is made up of four young rookies assigned to the motorcycle patrol and their leader, Lieutenant Briggs (Hal Holbrook). The physical characteristics of the four boyish and innocent-looking rookies and their distinguished leader give them a respectability and credibility that Dirty Harry cannot match.

The young death squad proceeds to eliminate a variety of stereo-typical villains until Callahan is assigned to investigate the killings — under Lieutenant Briggs's supervision. Callahan's first response to the murders is that it's all right with him. Yet when he discovers who it is that's doing the killing and confronts one of them, he begins by saying sarcastically, "You heroes have killed a dozen people this week." The vigilantes contend that they are the first generation that has learned to fight back, that they are simply ridding society of people that the courts would take care of if they worked. They conclude by saying, "It's not a question of *whether* to use violence; there's simply no other way." Ironically, this should be Callahan's speech, since it has been his basic *modus operandi*. But when they ask him to join them in distributing their justice, he simply replies that they have misjudged him. That said, the only solution to the conflict is the death of one side or the other. In the motion toward the movie's violent conclusion, Callahan's partner is killed, the rookies are killed, and Lieutenant Briggs is killed.

The conflict in *Magnum Force* places the maximum stress on the mythical structure of the Dirty Harry movies as Callahan comes face to face with his self-image in the rookies. Exactly how does Callahan see himself as different? Briggs admits that they are vigilantes, but he argues that evil demands evil. Callahan contends that the police can't be their own executioners. "I hate the system, but until someone comes along and makes some better changes, I'll stick with it." It doesn't exactly rank with the stature of Winston Churchill's remark about democracy, but it does serve to indicate where Harry draws the line. He's not an executioner; he just takes care of all the shit.

Mythically this movie underscores an important conflict in the profile of the solo savior. The world is evil, and since justice is perverted, there is no real way to save it. Even so, the demands of justice must be respected. The four rookies and Lieutenant Briggs have the trappings of civilization on their side. To all appearances they are trustworthy and reliable — everything Dirty Harry is not. But they have crossed the line between civilization and chaos that Harry continues to respect. He is willing to stand by justice even when it fails. Like the Duke on the western frontier, Dirty Harry in the jungle of San Francisco seeks to preserve that line in the hope that civilization will eventually emerge. Yet is this really a solution or mythical sleight of hand?

The Feminist Issue — *The Enforcer*

The Enforcer follows the formula established in the first two movies, although it is not nearly as good as *Dirty Harry*. The law is still in the hands of those who would placate criminals, and criminals are still odious (in this case, a group of pseudo-revolutionaries led by a sadistic homosexual). Unfortunately, the formula has become too pat and easy; the thrill is gone. Yet the film is to some extent redeemed by Tyne Daly's extremely good performance as Callahan's partner, Inspector Kate Moore. The Moore character introduces a new conflict into the series: the Duke mythology now has to cope not only with the new urban context but also with a liberated woman.[15]

Callahan first encounters Moore after he has been taken off homicide and assigned to personnel. As part of his new duties, he sits on an examining board to approve or deny department promotions and transfer requests. After having worked for ten years in records, Moore has applied for a promotion to the rank of Inspector (the same as Callahan). He

15. The Duke's own mythical confrontation with the liberated woman occurs in *Rooster Cogburn* (1975), costarring Katherine Hepburn.

ridicules her experience. She defends herself, but Callahan remains uncon-
vinced. In fact, he argues that no women should be assigned to field work,
and on that point gets into trouble with a representative of the mayor —
another woman. She argues that the police force should be brought into
the mainstream of the twentieth century and the Neanderthals should be
winnowed out. In the end, the mayor's representative prevails. Moore's
promotion is approved, and when Callahan is reassigned to homicide to
investigate the revolutionaries, Moore becomes his partner.

The real tension in the movie centers in the attempt to resolve the
conflict between Callahan and Moore at the mythological level. Can the
Duke accept a woman as a genuine partner — that is to say, as an equal?
Initially the conflict is played for laughs. Callahan acts like a stereotypical
sexist male, and Moore is earnest but naive, an intelligent female trying
to get ahead without the benefit of the male's experience. At the outset,
she does some things that appear to vindicate Callahan's opinion. For
example, at a demonstration of a portable rocket launcher, she stands
directly behind the weapon until Callahan pulls her out of harm's way at
the last minute. She makes a series of similar unprofessional mistakes, and
Harry repeatedly responds by saying "Marvelous," in his patented dead-
pan, sarcastic style. Yet, in their first real confrontation with revolutionaries, Moore is the first to spot the suspect, and she helps give chase.

Callahan's view of women does not begin to change until after he
has been fired from the police force for refusing to take part in a sham
ceremony. As he walks out, Moore follows him and promises to help him
in any way she can; she even implies that she is willing to bend the law
to do so. For the first time she calls him "Harry," and he calls her "Kate."
He asks her why she isn't married and raising a couple of kids. Standing
in the shadow of Coit Tower, she makes a joke about *coitus interruptus.*
The scene isn't played as seductive in any way, but it does serve to bring
Callahan and Moore closer together as two people who are learning to
care for and respect each other. This constitutes a significant dent in the
mythological armor of Dirty Harry.

Moore does manage to help Callahan. Her experience in records,
of which Harry had earlier been dismissive, proves to be valuable in
breaking the case open. The information she uncovers eventually leads
them to Alcatraz, where the revolutionaries have taken the mayor hostage.
Harry and Kate assault the island. In the inevitable concluding shoot-out,
she performs as well as Callahan, shooting one of the revolutionaries and
freeing the mayor. But when Harry gets caught in the cross fire, Moore

steps in and takes the bullet. Mortally wounded, she dies in Callahan's arms telling him to get her killer. "You can count on it," he promises.

What standard should we use to judge the relationship between Callahan and Moore? Certainly it falls short of a feminist standard of equality. While Callahan does eventually learn to relate to Moore as an equal, he does so only on his own terms. Moore has to pay a high price to gain his acceptance — not only her life but, to some extent, her integrity as a woman and as a police officer. She violates the rules of the system to help Harry, and in doing so she becomes dirty, too. And then she takes the stereotypical macho steps of entering the crossfire to take the bullet meant for Harry and then calling down vengeance on her killer. All of this is consistent with Dirty Harry's worldview, not Moore's. The film does demonstrate how a mythological structure can adapt to accept a new conflict, but it also suggests limitations to that adaptation. A women gains acceptance into the myth only by playing a role sanctioned by the myth. Still, the myth *is* altered, and lasting change is evident in Callahan: women play prominent roles in the next two movies in the series.

Revenge is Mine — *Sudden Impact*

Sudden Impact advances another problem in the moral calculus of the series. The plot spins out from an incident that took place ten years before the time in which the movie is set. Jennifer Spenser (Sondra Locke) and her sister Beth were gang raped under the boardwalk at Carmel. Beth was brutalized to the point that she fell into a coma and never regained consciousness. The local sheriff compounded the women's injuries by covering up the crime. Thus we have the classic context for a Dirty Harry movie: really bad criminals and a breakdown of justice.

The movie opens on a man and a woman necking in the front seat of a car. She unzips his fly, draws a chrome-plated revolver, and shoots him in the genitals. The woman is Jennifer. She later explains to her unresponsive sister that she had not been looking for their attackers when she caught sight of one of them on a street in San Francisco, but once she had seen him, she watched him for a few days and then let him pick her up in a bar. "He touched me, then I killed him. I love you, Beth."

Following her initial success, Spenser sets out on a program of systematic revenge. She returns to Carmel under the pretext of restoring a carousel there and begins to kill one gang member after another. Callahan, who is "vacationing" in Carmel, links the new murders there with the killing in San Francisco. Further investigation leads him to identify Spenser — with whom he has become involved — as the killer.

Callahan's relationship with Spenser is important on two counts: first, it marks a significant departure of the Dirty Harry character from his long-standing asceticism; second, it marks a significant perpetuation of the series ethos in the sense that Harry becomes attached to a woman who is much like himself — she, too, has been violated by the system.

The violent conclusion of *Sudden Impact* takes place at the amusement park on the same boardwalk where the gang rape had occurred ten years earlier. Kruger (Jack Thibeau), the particularly nasty gang leader, has taken Spenser to the park to kill her. "This time you'll have to rape my dead body," she says, fighting back as he beats her viciously. Then the camera provides a long shot: in the distance on the boardwalk, backlit, stands Dirty Harry with a huge gun at his side. As usual, there is no cavalry, but Callahan is there. And, as usual, the fight is to the death. Harry repeats the now-famous epithet "Make my day" and shoots Kruger, who falls through the roof of the carousel and is impaled on the horn of the unicorn — a fitting enough punishment for his crime.

As the police are removing the bodies, Spenser asks Harry what happens next. What about justice? A young officer comes over and says that they found a .38 in Kruger's belt. Callahan tells him that when they check the ballistics, they'll find that it's the same gun used in the killings. He says nothing about the fact that the gun belongs to Spenser.

There are multiple ironies in Callahan's decision not to turn Spenser in. For one thing, Harry has always sneered at psychologists and sociologists that he believes cater to criminals, and yet in this case he subscribes to a psychological explanation of Spenser's acts — or at least he grants her a reprieve from punishment on psychological grounds. He decides that she has acted not simply out of revenge but out of compulsion. The state of her comatose sister provides a clue to her own psychological state. Throughout the movie, Spenser paints a ghastly, haunted self-portrait. Even though Harry recognizes this as one of the clues that she is the killer, he spends the night with her. So his decision to let her go free is not simply his way of letting true justice work its way out. Callahan is not joining the rookies in *Magnum Force* and helping to execute those who have done evil; to the contrary, by letting Spenser go he is preventing justice from taking its full course. He has decided that in this case, the law-and-order mentality will not suffice. Considerations of Spenser's psychological state override considerations of the letter of the law and thereby alter the established moral calculus of the series. In a real sense, the fate of this woman disassembles a part of the Dirty Harry mythology.

Your Number Is Up — *The Dead Pool*

The final episode (I hope) in the Dirty Harry series is *The Dead Pool*. This film continues to follow the increasingly threadbare series formula, albeit with some new developments along a couple of lines — Callahan's relationship with women and the moral calculus associated with the victim, which in this case includes Callahan himself. The plot centers on the production of a horror movie. Yet another psychopathic killer is on the loose, and during the filming of their movie, the director and several of his production assistants are playing a macabre game involving lists of people they think will be victims of the killer during the course of the filming — the "dead pool." The killer, a man named Rook (David Hunt) gains access to the director's list and begins killing all the people on it, thereby rendering the director a chief suspect. Callahan's name turns up on the director's list, and he is assigned to investigate the case.

The female interest in the story is Samantha Walker (Sondra Locke), who automatically earns Callahan's contempt because of her profession: she's a TV reporter. The movie portrays all members of the media as vultures who descend on crime scenes to pick the bones dry. They interfere with police investigations, and they are not interested in justice but only the story, in sensationalism. Walker is involved in the story in two ways: (1) the killer chooses to send her important clues, and (2) she wants to do a story on Inspector Callahan. So there are two people pursuing Callahan in this movie: the killer and Samantha Walker. In many respects, Walker poses the greater threat to Callahan. He has dealt with psychopaths before and has always triumphed, but Walker is seeking to get beneath his facade, to strip away the sunglasses he hides behind.

The development of the relationship between Callahan and Walker is more interesting than his detective work. They first meet as Callahan arrives to investigate the murder of a rock star. When the victim's girlfriend arrives in an obvious state of distress, the television reporters swarm all over her. Callahan comes to her rescue, trashing one of the cameras in the process. Walker threatens a lawsuit but says she'll drop it if Harry agrees to have dinner with her. Under pressure from his superiors, he agrees. Over dinner Walker proposes to do an in-depth story on him, but he refuses. "All you are interested in is blood," he says. The sentiment is echoed when, at the burial of the rock star, Callahan confronts the director, who at that time is a suspect. When asked about whether there is any relation between his movies and the dead pool murder, the director says, "People are fascinated with death and violence."

Callahan rejects TV news on the grounds that it is only interested in blood, and he is contemptuous of the director's glib assertion that people are fascinated with death and violence; yet both the Dirty Harry character and the Dirty Harry movies are built on the truth of these propositions. The constant mayhem in these films is one of their chief attractions. Audience interest grows along with the body count. In any event, *The Dead Pool* concludes as other Dirty Harry movies do — with a chase and a death. To the background music of "Welcome to the Jungle," Rook threatens to kill Callahan with his own gun. Just when he thinks he has cornered his quarry, however, Harry appears behind him, silhouetted against the light, and announces, "You're out of bullets" — a clear echo of the opening scene of the first Dirty Harry movie, in which Harry asks the bank robber whether he thinks the gun is empty. He then tells Rook, "You're shit out of luck," repeating the line he had used earlier in the movie, in the formulaic opening confrontation in the Chinese restaurant. And then he kills his would-be killer by impaling him with a harpoon. The movie closes with an overhead shot of Callahan and Walker leaving the scene as police officers and television reporters swarm over Rook's dead body. Harry has won on two accounts: he got the killer, and he kept Walker from getting her story.

And yet *The Dead Pool* violates the Dirty Harry myth. If the gun was empty, there was no need for Callahan to kill the villain. When he chose to do so anyway, he finally did join the rookies from *Magnum Force:* he became an executioner. It would seem that the purpose of *The Dead Pool* was not so much to demythologize the myth of the solo savior as it was to use the audience's fascination with violence and death to mislead it into reaffirming the myth in a new guise.[16] The world presented

16. John G. Cawelti has listed four ways in which recent films have transformed genre: (1) burlesque *(Blazing Saddles)*, (2) nostalgia *(True Grit, Raiders of the Lost Ark)*, (3) demythologization *(Chinatown, Bonnie and Clyde)*, and (4) the affirmation of myth for

throughout the series is so evil, so irrational, so unrational that the hero can always plausibly establish some new moral line to separate himself from the evil. The original mutation of the John Wayne hero was precipitated by a shift from the wide open spaces to the urban world. But any such paradigm shift calls for an associated reordering of the moral space. The Dirty Harry movies keep searching for that line, but the line keeps moving. In the end, Callahan runs out of ways to reformulate the moral calculus, and the myth collapses in on itself. The driving force of the myth is the need to preserve justice, to overcome evil, to protect "life, liberty, and the pursuit of happiness," but in his efforts to do so, Callahan finally violates justice and indulges in evil himself. Harry becomes judge and executioner, and we in the audience scarcely notice. We have become so fascinated with violence in its own right that in the end we consent to the assertion that it is the price we will have to pay to preserve life and liberty. On this level, the myth can be said still to work — as long as we don't ask too many embarrassing questions.

The Wild West Show

It is unfair to the work of Clint Eastwood to represent him only as the maker of violent movies. The Eastwood persona, developed not only in the Dirty Harry cycle but also in the spaghetti Westerns and other films, is like the John Wayne persona — larger than life — and it obscures other capabilities of the actor. Beginning with *Play Misty for Me* (1971) and including the recent *Bird* (1988), Eastwood has made a number of fine films, some of which are at variance with the core myth. The most obvious example is *Bronco Billy* (1980). This movie, made right in the middle of the Dirty Harry cycle, shows the positive side of the western myth while rejecting the Dirty Harry stereotype.[17]

---

its own sake. Speaking of the fourth category, he says, "In films in this mode, a traditional genre and its myth are probed and shown to be unreal, but then the myth itself is at least partially affirmed as a reflection of authentic human aspirations and needs" ("*Chinatown* and Generic Transformation in Recent American Films," in *Film Genre Reader*, ed. Barry Keith Grant [Austin: University of Texas Press, 1986], pp. 192-99). He cites *The Wild Bunch* as an example; I would add the Dirty Harry cycle.

     17. In terms of Cawelti's schema, *Bronco Billy* belongs to group three: it demythologizes.

The scale of this movie is different from that of the Dirty Harry cycle; it's small and quiet, with an atmosphere that is reassuring rather than threatening. This is not to say that the characters are not threatened — they are — but throughout the movie there is a sense of hope however desperate things become. Observing the differences between the films tells us much about the other side of the solo savior.

The plot is almost irrelevant to the movie's mythical development. It is a throwback to the zany comedies of the 1930s. Antoinette Lilly (Sondra Locke), an extremely rich and spoiled woman, has married a man simply to inherit her father's estate, but her new husband promptly abandons her with literally nothing somewhere in the middle of Montana. She falls in with the Bronco Billy Wild West Show, a ragtag group of performers who travel the small-town circuit playing mostly to audiences of children. Miss Lilly offers ample evidence of her disdain for the Wild West show from the outset. She joins the group as a way of returning to civilization. Billy and his group are unaware of her wealth and accept her into their midst out of pity. Just when she is ready to leave the group, she spots a newspaper headline announcing that she has been murdered and that her husband has been convicted of the crime. He had agreed with the family lawyer to plead insanity in exchange for a short prison term and a payoff of $500,000. All goes well until the Bronco Billy show stops at an asylum for the criminally ill where the incarcerated husband is being held. He spots his wife and blows the whistle, leading to the denouement and eventual reconciliation.

In this movie, the whole is greater than the sum of its parts. The Bronco Billy Wild West Show is a small-time outfit that is perpetually broke. Most of its members are ex-convicts that Billy met while he, too, was serving time. Billy has a fairly nice riding and shooting act, but it's exactly the same every night. He gets upset whenever his female partner deviates even by one word from the script. Chief Big Eagle (Dan Vadis), who is writing the "great American Indian novel" at night, does a snake dance in the show. Billy buys him harmless gopher snakes for the act, but the Chief insists on using real rattlesnakes even though they keep biting him. Billy fumes in frustration with the proud man and finally says, "The only good Indian is a dead Indian" — but it is a gruff expression of his affection for the man. As individuals the performers in the group fail, but as a group they heal.

An early scene sets the tone for this counterpoint between group and individual. The group is traveling to another show when Doc (Scatman Crothers), Billy's sidekick and the group's spokesman, reminds Billy that it's been six months since the group has been paid. They don't make much money at the best of their stops, and they're often putting on free shows for orphanages and asylums — for the sort of dispossessed, forgotten, broken people that they themselves are. Billy stops the truck in disgust and charges the group with disloyalty. He listens to their complaints: Lefty (Bill McKinney) needs a new hand to replace his hook, Leonard (Sam Bottoms) needs some new ropes for his roping act, and Big Eagle and his wife, Running Water (Sierra Pecheur), need a new bed. Billy answers each complaint with a put-down along the lines of his put-down of Big Eagle ("The only good Indian . . ."). The whole scene plays ironically against the western myth: Bronco Billy puts on his best tough man act, the lone hero, and yet there he is presiding over a run-down show and a collection of variously damaged human beings. The complainers all begin to regret having provoked the boss, and Billy concludes the matter by invoking the group's sustaining dream: "Someday we'll get enough money to buy a ranch so city kids can see what cowboys were really like." This goal serves an eschatological function for the group throughout the movie. It's what the Wild West Show is all about.

Miss Lilly provides the outsider's perspective on the seriocomic menagerie. She instinctively focuses on how broken the performers are as individuals, but over time she cannot help but see how happy they are as a group. Several scenes play on the distance between Miss Lilly and the group. The members of the troop try to be nice to her, even though she never returns the favor, because they think she is down on her luck and depressed about her husband having abandoned her. Her constant put-downs are hard to take, however. While at a bar celebrating the announcement of the impending birth of a baby to Big Eagle and Running Water, Billy asks her if she has ever considered what it might be like to be nice to people. "People only want to take," she says. Then she leaves the bar alone and meets up with some men who attempt to rape her until Billy and the group come to her rescue. For the first time she begins to see the importance of group solidarity.

Miss Lilly begins to see the meaning of the Wild West Show. At one point, Billy confesses to her that he had served seven years for attempting to murder his wife after he found her in bed with his best friend. "You tried to kill your wife?" she asks incredulously. Of course he tried to kill his wife, he says; after all, the man was his best friend. In a Dirty Harry movie this would be one of those lines in which Harry establishes his aloofness from the sort of intimate bonding characteristic of relation-ships with women and his preference for the cooler, more detached con-nections of simple friendship. But Bronco Billy is not Dirty Harry. Miss Lilly has seen the love within the troop and has begun to appreciate Billy as a gentle, if daffy, soul. She also finds out that before he went to prison and then on to become the leader of the Wild West show, he was a shoe salesman in New Jersey — yet another undercutting of the western myth. When she asks him if he's for real, he says, significantly, "I'm who I want to be." This theme plays out further as Miss Lilly seeks to resist the inevitable romance that is developing between her and Billy. The turning point comes when Running Water says to her, "Don't you know what Bronco Billy and the Wild West Show are all about? You can be anything you want. All you have to do is go out and do it." A shoe salesman can become a cowboy, and Miss Lilly can find love and happiness.

But the real world keeps intruding into the Wild West Show. When their tent burns down, the troupe draws on its informing myth and decides to rob a train. Miss Lilly protests that this is the real world, that people could get killed, that there aren't any more cowboys and Indians. But they charge off after the train anyway — and meet another sort of reality: the train speeds on and ignores them altogether. The only success they have is in bringing some ironic joy to the only witness of their attempted robbery, a little boy looking out the window who sees cowboys and Indians chasing the train. In another scene Leonard, the young roper, gets arrested, and it's discovered that he's a Vietnam deserter. As a consequence, he is brutalized by the deputies. Even Bronco Billy denounces him as being unfit to be in the Wild West Show: he's a poor example for "our little partners." Yet Billy takes what money he has been able to squirrel away and offers the sheriff a bribe to let Leonard go. The sheriff takes the bribe, but in a scene patterned on the old-fashioned shoot-out, he insists on humiliating Billy by making him say that the sheriff is a faster draw than he is. When Billy complies, the sheriff sneers that he's "nothing but a yellow belly egg sucker." But in both these scenes the conclusion is the same: the group stays together. Even though Billy disapproves of Leonard's past behavior, and especially his having kept it secret, he spends the money the group has been saving to buy a ranch in order to restore Leonard to their fellowship. The established order remains uni-formly hostile, but there is love and help to be found among the marginal-ized. When the group goes to the insane asylum it has frequented over the years, the inmates provide them with a new tent constructed out the American flags the inmates produce there.

The movie closes predictably with the conversion of Miss Lilly. She parts ways with the Wild West show and returns to her penthouse in New York. Alone there, she swallows a bottle of sleeping tablets. But then the phone rings. It's Running Water calling to tell her that Billy needs her. She spits out the pills. The suicide attempt, like much else with Miss Lilly, was a front.

The Solo Savior Myth

Though both *Bronco Billy* and the Dirty Harry cycle are grounded in the solo savior myth, they deal with it in quite different ways. The Dirty Harry movies reinforce the myth by increasing the fascination with violence; *Bronco Billy* subverts the myth by burlesquing it. None of these movies appeals to a divine figure. Yet the structure of their fictional worlds implies a great deal about God (or the absence of God).

Often the Dirty Harry movies have been seen by critics as apologetics for right-wing, anti-liberal ideologies, but that misses the point. They draw on a common fear in urban America — namely, that the system doesn't work. Urban dwellers feel themselves to be at risk from a thousand nameless and unpredictable threats. They live in fear and view their world as evil and hostile. The Dirty Harry films take this view of the world to an extreme by suggesting that the situation is irredeemable. Harry must stand alone against the evil, as even the system of justice and the police force align themselves against him. On occasion, the embattled solo savior feels it necessary to cross the line into lawlessness to preserve justice, although this is a gray area, since the films are constantly redrawing that line and redefining justice.

One of the primary functions of savior myths is to provide a sense of redemption. Abstractly, redemption is the resolution of a fundamental conflict that is separating some individual or group from a desired object. The savior serves to bridge the gap. Unfortunately, many discussions of redemption fail to deal adequately with the issue of what one is being redeemed *from* and *for* — an issue that is critical for the definition of the savior's role. In the Dirty Harry cycle, the conflict is created by the world, which is a place of evil. But the films fall short of a classic dualism because they fail to offer any clear anti-pole, any good principle to counter the evil world; there is no promise of a heaven to which one can escape from this veil of tears. In fact, the savior figure in these films occasionally indulges in some of the very lawlessness that he ostensibly finds so repulsive. The films end up conveying the message that the solution to the problem of evil is overwhelming violence. Again and again, Callahan's violence is effective in temporarily holding the evil at bay and producing a more or less satisfying catharsis — really a fleeting illusion of redemption.

Bronco Billy dramatizes what Dirty Harry lacks — a sense of community and eschatology, a beneficent present and a future that engenders some hope. Harry stands essentially alone in an evil world. He lost his wife, he loses his partners to death or resignation, and he is the target of perpetual random violence himself. The best alliances Callahan manages to form prove to be only temporary. The world of *Bronco Billy* is likewise beset by evil and betrayal — by would-be rapists and corrupt sheriffs — but it never appears to be irredeemable. Each character in the movie is clearly flawed and remains flawed, and yet they are all provided with the opportunity to be whatever they want, to be redeemed. The Wild West Show is not an open-air asylum for the self-deluded, as Miss Lilly mistakenly believes. It is a place where flawed people become more than themselves by reaching out to empower one another as well as others outside the group. Even their most specific eschatological hope encompasses not only themselves but others: they are united in the dream of a ranch where the little partners can see what real cowboys and Indians were like.

Romans 5–8

Film is an essentially concrete rather than abstract medium. And because one person's vision of such abstractions as community, freedom, and eschatology may vary considerably from another person's, it may not always be easy for Christians to recognize such cherished virtues when they are depicted in specific images on the screen. I would like to spend some time, then, looking how the apostle Paul's vision of community, freedom, and eschatology compares with corresponding visions in *Bronco Billy* and the Dirty Harry cycle.

Although there are important and telling differences between the anthropology implicit in Paul's writing and the anthropology implicit in the Dirty Harry movies, there are also points at which they are not all that far apart. Harry views the world, its systems, and those in it as evil, and

Paul agrees that humans are weak, ungodly, and sinners (Rom. 8:6-7). But Harry views the human situation as irredeemable. He may be able to stave off disaster for the moment, but he holds out no hope for any sort of larger or more lasting redemption. In the Dirty Harry movies, as in most apocalyptic texts (e.g., Mark 13), vigilance is a virtue, and yet in these films it is not connected to any ultimate redeemer or solution. Vengeance is presented as the only satisfying response for human beings caught in a web of systemic evil.

Paul takes a somewhat different tack. For our purposes, Romans 5:6 can be said to summarize his position: "While we were still weak, at the right time Christ died for the ungodly." "While we were still weak" — that is to say, before humanity received faith, when it was godless, in a state that is essentially equivalent to Dirty Harry's perception of it — precisely then was the "right time," the appropriate time (καιρός), for Christ to die for weak sinners.[18] This same thought is repeated in the parallel formulation of verse 8 — "But God shows his love for us in that while we were still sinners Christ died for us" (NRSV). This sets up a paradox in which the "still" binds together the opposites of the love of God and our ungodliness.[19] This goes to the heart of the essential difference between Dirty Harry and Paul. As Harry sees it, it is the world's ungodliness that accounts for its irredeemability: there is nothing in it to love. Paul, on the other hand, affirms God's paradoxical love for the ungodly. Paul does not resort here to the cliche of hating the sin and loving the sinner. That misses the power of what he is proposing. God, he says, loves those who are "still sinners." He even underscores the paradox by arguing that few of us would be prepared to die even for a righteous person, much less for an ungodly one (v. 7). The solution to the problem of evil according to both Dirty Harry and Paul involves violence, although in the Dirty Harry movies the violence is a continuing spasm of revenge, whereas Paul characterizes Jesus' death as an act of love "on our behalf" (ὑπὲρ ἡμῶν).

The power of evil in the human community is an important theme

18. "Still" appears twice in the verse. Many manuscripts omit the second "still," since it makes no apparent grammatical sense, but the repetition does serve to underscore the urgency of the term. "Whether it originated as a primitive error in the exemplar of the first collection of the Pauline Letters, or whether it arose when, as one may assume, Paul repeated ἔτι, perhaps for the sake of emphasis . . . it is impossible to say" (*A Textual Commentary on the Greek New Testament*, ed. Bruce Metzger [New York: United Bible Societies, 1971], p. 512).

19. The paradox is further revealed by the question it provokes in the imaginary dialogue that follows: "Should we continue to sin in order that grace may abound?" (Rom. 6:1).

in both the Dirty Harry movies and the writings of Paul. In the Dirty Harry cycle, people are possessed and driven by evil; the whole system is corrupt. Moreover, the evil is essentially inexplicable. Such explanations as are offered — psychological and sociological — are dismissed by Callahan with contempt. They serve no good purpose; in fact, they provide a rationale for coddling criminals, nurturing yet more evil. Paul also views evil as inexplicable: "I do not understand my own actions. For I do not do what I want, but I do the very thing I hate. . . . It is no longer I that do it, but sin which dwells within me" (Rom. 7:15, 17). But there are also differences between Paul and Dirty Harry at this point. For one thing, Paul speaks in the first person (representing all human beings as well as himself when he does so), whereas Dirty Harry indicts the rest of the world from behind his sunglasses but exempts himself from the judgment.[20] More importantly, Paul moves beyond the problem, positing a solution that is equally inexplicable: while humans are still ungodly, acting under the dominance of sin, God demonstrates love for them. When he seeks to do good, he encounters the mystery that evil is close at hand (Rom. 7:21); having come to faith, he encounters a greater mystery: "I have been crucified with Christ; it is no longer I who live, but Christ who lives in me" (Gal. 2:20). Harry remains trapped because he is unable to look beyond himself for a solution. Paul understands that we will remain trapped in our evil until we acknowledge the one true power beyond ourselves. Indeed, if we seek to do good on our own, we will inevitably find that evil lies close at hand, because in seeking to do the good we risk setting ourselves up as God. Harry falls into this trap. In each of the movies, he makes himself responsible for determining the moral line. He keeps trying to distinguish his own actions from those of the criminals he pursues, but in the end he cannot do so: he becomes the executioner, and we see that he has been the executioner all along. Harry is the perfect example of an individual "under the law." "I find it to be a law that when I want to do right, evil lies close at hand" (Rom. 7:21).

Paul recognizes that our desire to do good is what seduces us into captivity to the law (Rom. 7:11). If anything, Paul's perception of the ubiquity of evil is more profound than Harry's, since Paul asserts that even

---

20. The character that Eastwood plays in *Tightrope* is a good deal more interesting in this regard. He is a police detective not unlike Dirty Harry, but he is shown to have proclivities similar to those of the criminal he is tracking down, and by rights he himself should be one of the suspects.

one's efforts to do good can lead to sin. Clearly Paul is torn. On the one hand he experiences a "delight in the law of God, in my inmost being" (v. 22), but on the other hand "I see in my members another law at war with the law of my mind and making me captive to the law of sin which dwells in my members" (v. 23). He calls himself a wretched man (v. 24) and concludes that "I of myself serve the the law of God with my mind, but with my flesh I serve the law of sin" (v. 25). But immediately following this extremely negative view of human existence, he states that "there is therefore now no condemnation for those who are in Christ Jesus" (8:1). How are we to reconcile Paul's assertion that he remains a slave to the law of sin with his assertion that now there is no condemnation? What happens to the struggle, the battle that underpins the plot of the Dirty Harry movies? One could construct an antinomian interpretation — which is apparently what the Corinthians did (1 Cor. 6:12). But Paul's point is not antinomian. He asserts elsewhere that God has "passed over former sins" (Rom. 3:25) or has elected not to "reckon" sin against us (4:8).

The death of Jesus creates for those in faith a field of action in which there is great freedom, growing out of the freedom from condemnation. And in the community of those in faith, the whole is greater than the sum of the parts, as indicated by Paul's image of the body of Christ. Those who acknowledge that it is no longer they who act but Christ who acts enter a community in which no single member stands alone. *Bronco Billy* presents an interesting example of the sort of community Paul is talking about. Like members of the Pauline communities, the members of the Wild West Show are far from perfect. They are flawed human beings, at war with other members of the community and with themselves. Even so, within the group they are given the freedom granted by acceptance to be whatever they want to be, as Running Water explains to Miss Lilly. Acceptance within the group confers freedom. Paul expresses a similar notion when he notes that "in everything God works for good with those who love him" (8:28). This leads Paul to ask, "If God is for us, who is against us?" (8:31). This is not to say that this freedom comes without a cost. In the very next verse, Paul acknowledges that God "did not spare his own Son but gave him up for us all." Likewise, Billy had to pay a high price to purchase Leonard's freedom — accepting humiliation from the sheriff. Significantly, though, the sort of violence that Billy suffers to redeem Leonard is different from Dirty Harry's kind of violence: it's sacrifice, not vengeance.

One of the most depressing aspects of the Dirty Harry vision of reality is that it holds no hope for the future; there is no end to the garbage Harry has to deal with. Bronco Billy's Wild West Show, on the other hand, is charged with hope for the future — specifically, the ranch that the members of the group dream of buying. Regardless of how unrealistic or childish this dream may be from the viewer's perspective, it does serve to infuse the group with hope and purpose. Paul, too, speaks often of a future hope based on an apocalyptic model. Yet it is as important to notice what Paul does *not* say about this future as what he does say about it. He engages in little speculation about the specific shape of the future life, for example; he offers no final judgment scenes, no scenes or promises of apocalyptic destruction of the world or evildoers.[21] Rather, he speaks most often of transformation.[22] He also links the believer with the whole of creation. Creation has been subjected to futility, is groaning as though it were in labor, awaiting the revelation of the children of God (Rom. 8:19-22). Creation itself is caught up in eschatological hope along with the believer; it is not a thing apart from the believer but rather "the setting of human history."[23] Creation groans together with the believer, awaiting redemption (v. 23).

In this regard, the vision of *Bronco Billy* is much closer to Paul's vision than is that of the Dirty Harry movies. After each setback for the Wild West Show, Billy reiterates their eschatological purpose. So, too, Paul: "I consider that the sufferings of this present time are not worth comparing with the glory that is to be revealed to us" (Rom. 8:18). Both Paul and Billy have a future because they have hope, a dream. Eschatology is a type of dream, as witness the dreamlike language of much of apocalyptic. Dreams are powerful phenomena and should not simply be dismissed as wishful thinking. Martin Luther King Jr. said, "I have a dream," and in many ways that dream changed a nation. The power of a dream lies in its ability to create a new present in anticipation of a future. The trick is to avoid political anaesthesia on the one hand and utopian fantasies on the other.

Given the level of anxiety in our culture today, both political anaesthesia and utopian fantasies are powerful temptations. Many people in

21. The closest Paul gets to the war mythology of apocalyptic is 1 Thess. 4:16: "For the Lord himself, with the archangel's call and with the sound of God's trumpet, will descend from heaven, and the dead in Christ will rise first."

22. See, e.g., 1 Cor. 14:51-52, where Paul teases the Corinthians with a mystery.

23. For a discussion of creation in the writings of Paul generally and this passage specifically, see Ernst Käsemann, *Commentary on Romans* (Grand Rapids: William B. Eerdmans, 1980), pp. 232ff.

urban America share the vision of life offered in the Dirty Harry movies — they feel thoroughly alienated and dread the threat of random violence. Many of these people long for someone out there to strike back at the bad guys who are threatening them. Dirty Harry feeds on this urban anxiety. The gritty realism and violence of the Dirty Harry movies and their even more violent successors (e.g., *Robocop, Lethal Weapon*) give some indication of the price we would have to pay if we were actually to adopt their solutions, but not everyone pays attention to this warning. Large numbers of us are drawn to the image of an avenging savior, the icon of the political strongman who is able and willing to meet violence with violence. Ronald Reagan rose to power on the strength of his vision of America standing tall (at one point he even used one of Dirty Harry's best-known lines, "Make my day"), and George Bush enjoyed unprecedented popularity when he overcame the perception that he was a wimp by facing down Saddam Hussein. After years of a sense of helplessness at the hands of the world's thugs, America appears to have been hungry for the fantasy of revenge. And many who disavowed that fantasy seemed willing to buy into the other side of the dream — the utopian fantasy, the hope of a fairy-tale ending, the belief that everything would be O.K. by the final reel. This is often the religious option — a belief that in the end God will make everything better, like a mother kissing away the hurt in her child's bruised knee.

What, then, are we to make of Paul's dream of a restored creation, Bronco Billy's dream of a ranch, and Martin Luther King Jr.'s dream of an America in which blacks and whites dwell together in harmony? Are they simply utopian fantasies? Yes, they are — for those who use them as a narcotic to prevent their having to deal with present trials and sufferings. But no, they are not fantasies for those who use the dreams to infuse their present with meaning and purpose. Not just any meaning or purpose will do, of course: it has to be the purpose of service to others, a meaning in which the whole is greater than the sum of the parts. Viewers may be inclined to dismiss Bronco Billy's dream as childish, but to such belong the kingdom. Bronco Billy reminds us in vivid images that the body of Christ may well look childish (as Jesus says) or foolish (as Paul says). "For Jews demand signs and Greeks seek wisdom" (1 Cor. 1:22) — and Americans want vengeance.

How do we conceive of God? As a cleaned-up Dirty Harry who will right all wrongs and defend our use of power (violence)? Or as Bronco Billy, the slightly daffy head of a community of flawed people devoted to the service of others?

Dirty Harry in Church

Having come this far, perhaps we should ask what validity all of this has for our understanding of the word of God. Does Dirty Harry really have anything worthwhile to say to the Christian community? Should he be admitted to the pulpit? Clearly the Dirty Harry films are not examples of the highest cinematic achievement. They are mass entertainment. Moreover, a steady diet of Dirty Harry films and others like them can be demoralizing if not amoralizing. Even so, I contend that the type of analysis we have engaged in is imperative for a revitalization and reformulation of preaching.

Medium and Message

Marshall McLuhan is perhaps best identified with the seemingly oxymoronic notion of the "global village" and with the gnomic assertion that "the medium is the message." The insights associated with these two phrases go a long way in explaining our current situation. The global village has arisen as we have moved from a principal dependence on print media to a principal dependence on electronic media for conserving our knowledge. As the world becomes more closely wired together, information travels faster, and differences begin to break down. The effects of this shift from print to electronic media involve more than just a faster production and distribution of information, a greater sense of interrelation, and a greater sense that the world is shrinking. As McLuhan's second slogan suggests, the change in the media is also producing a change in the message. A culture in which the printing press is preeminent will tend to view texts as fixed, because the press produces an almost limitless number of identical texts. In the area of biblical studies, this presumption of fixity of the text led to the rise of textual criticism, the attempt to establish the original text of the Bible; it is now generally conceded that this goal is unreachable. In the area of biblical interpretation, the presumption of the fixity of the text led to the rise of historical criticism, the attempt to establish the meaning of a text by identifying the original author's intention; this goal, too, has been widely abandoned. Ironically, the approach of the fundamentalists, who pride themselves on having rejected historical criticism in deference to the Bible's literal meaning, is itself clearly a product of era of the printing press in the extent to which it affirms the complete fixity and preeminence of the biblical text. But fundamentalists overlook the fact that if the text is indeed fixed, then it can be compared with other texts, with the result that differences unrecognized in earlier harmonizations of oral traditions will begin to appear — and such differences demand historical interpretation.

As dominance has shifted from print media to electronic media, the message has changed.[24] In an electronic culture, text is composed of images and sound. Indeed, we live in an environment bombarded by sound and pictures, and we are only beginning to realize how this is affecting literacy, the great by-product of the printing press.[25] The symptoms of this shift from print to images and sound are all around us — falling SAT scores, shorter attention spans, the electronic church, electronic journalism, political campaign debates condensed into a series of thirty-second sound bites, and so on.[26]

This electronic environment now is causing rapid shifts in biblical studies and homiletics as well.[27] The rise of literary criticism and various narrative theologies is likewise a symptom of the shift. These approaches characteristically deal with the texts as a whole, rather than in the fragmentary fashion of liturgical tradition. A homiletics born in the age of the

24. In saying that the dominance has shifted from print to electronic media, I am in no way saying that print is no longer important. I am simply noting the ascendancy of the visual. More people now get their news from television than from newspapers, and even the newspapers have changed to emulate electronic media — perhaps most notably *USA Today*.

25. In 1969 Neil Postman wrote a book entitled *Teaching as a Subversive Activity* (New York: Delacorte Press), arguing, as the title suggests, that the purpose of education is to subvert the establishment. But ten years later he had become so alarmed by the influence of television that he wrote *Teaching as a Conserving Activity* (New York: Delacorte Press, 1979), arguing that the purpose of education should be to preserve the fruits of the printing press.

26. The literature on the effects of TV and advertising on the political process is enormous. For an excellent study of the manipulation of the media by the White House, see Mark Hertsgaard, *On Bended Knee: The Press and the Reagan Presidency* (New York: Schocken Books, 1989). For an interesting analysis of the formative influence of radio and the movies on Ronald Reagan's perception of the world, see Gary Wills, *Reagan's America: Innocents at Home* (Garden City, N.Y.: Doubleday, 1987).

27. David Buttrick's *Homiletic: Moves and Structures* (Philadelphia: Fortress Press, 1987) reflects the beginnings of these shifts. Just notice the titles of the initial chapters: "Moves," "Framework," "Images," and "Language." The metaphors are drawn from literary criticism and film direction, not from traditional theology.

Reformation and the printing press is in serious jeopardy.[28] There is increasing pressure to stress the performance aspects of preaching and liturgy, especially in the mega-churches.[29]

Hermeneutics as Conversation

Traditional hermeneutics has utilized the metaphor of translation. Crudely put, the hermeneutical task has been conceived as translating the essence, truth, and the like of a text into modern terms.[30] Bultmann's program of demythologization is a sophisticated example of this model. New Testament mythology is translated into existential categories compatible with and understandable to the modern mind. The problem with this model is its assumption that the translation can take place without substantial loss. In order to translate, one must first determine what the text means, which means that the interpreter has to start from a privileged position, with a prior knowledge of what needs to be translated and what does not. Or to put it another way, the program of demythologization depends on the ability of the interpreter to shed his or her subjectivity. Moreover, the program is opaque to the fact that a shift in medium entails a shift in message. The recent development of strategies of polyvalency implicitly relativizes the fixity of the text.

It has not been my intent in this essay to try to translate Paul into the image of post-modernity. Rather, I have tried to set up a conversation between Paul on the one hand and Dirty Harry and Bronco Billy, as variations on the American solo savior myth, on the other, in the hope that they will be mutually illuminating. The advantage of this sort of *conversation* is that it promotes mutuality, a common search for truth, while recognizing the ambiguity and plurality of our situation. Conversa-

28. The classic study of the relation between the printing press and the Protestant Reformation is Elizabeth L. Eisenstein's *The Printing Press as an Agent of Change, Communications and Cultural Transformation in Early Modern Europe,* 2 vols. (New York: Cambridge University Press, 1979).

29. An excerpt from a recent article (Cindy Lafavre Yorks, "McChurch," *USA Weekend,* 13-15 April 1990, p. 4) says it all: "To attract churchgoers today, you've got to please the consumer. That means high-tech entertainment."

30. George Lakoff and Mark Johnson describe this as the "conduit metaphor"; see *Metaphors We Live By* (Chicago: University of Chicago Press, 1980), pp. 10-13.

tion "is not a confrontation," says David Tracy. "It is not a debate. It is not an exam. It is questioning itself. It is a willingness to follow the question wherever it may go. It is dialogue."[31] By engaging Paul and Dirty Harry as partners in conversation, we can follow out the questions they are asking, even when those questions are unexpressed. By creating a conversation between two such apparently disparate characters, we allow each to appear in a new configuration in the conversational horizon of the other. In conversation "we notice that to attend to the other as other, the different as different, is also to understand the different *as* possible."[32] Because we are engaging in a conversation, we can learn both to hear and to speak in different ways.

Myth — The Hidden Conversation

In setting up this conversation, I chose to engage both Paul and Dirty Harry at the mythological level. This strategy was explicit and deliberate, aimed at addressing several concerns. Perhaps most basically, my concern in establishing the ground rules of the conversation was to show that if we are not aware of our own mythological structures, then when we invoke structures in biblical narrative that are similar to those in contemporary discourse, we may unwittingly substitute the contemporary myth for the ancient. It is precisely in this way that the mind creates a homeostasis,[33] rendering the ancient contemporaneous, rendering the foreign familiar, and thus making revelation routine. While fundamentalist discourse takes this track under the banner of literalism, a more refined homiletics runs the same risk if it is unaware of its own contemporaneous mythological structures. A homiletics unaware of its mythological commitments is a homiletics whose guiding hand is hidden.

This understanding of myth has two important implications for homiletics. First, while the emphasis on storytelling in recent theology is commendable, if it is pursued apart from an analysis of contemporary narratives, the ancient story may become only a matter of antiquarian

31. Tracy, *Plurality and Ambiguity: Religion as a Test Case for Hermeneutics* (San Francisco: Harper & Row, 1987), p. 19.

32. Tracy, *Plurality and Ambiguity*, p. 20.

33. See Walter Ong, *Orality and Literacy: The Technologizing of the Word* (New York: Methuen, 1982), pp. 46-69.

interest, or a matter of romantic reinvestment, or it may be inappropriately updated to fit the needs of modern myth. Second, we will be missing the point if we employ movies merely as examples in homilies. Certainly we would miss the real strength of these movies if we were to use them in this way, and we would also run a significant risk of misleading the audience. By appealing to the movie as example, the homilist may unwittingly introduce a mythological structure at variance with that of the biblical text, but it is even more likely that he or she will miss the opportunity to explore the movie as an example of contemporary mythology.

In closing, I should note that there are also risks associated with successfully bringing film and biblical text into conversation with one another. Theological categories are incarnated through narrative imaging. Such enfleshment may well take us off guard at first — as, for example, in the juxtaposition of Paul and Dirty Harry. It is much less threatening to speak abstractly of a preferential option for the poor than it is to deal with the image of Bronco Billy's Wild West Show. Such an image not only pictures for us a mixed community (a favorite theme of Matthew's Gospel) but also challenges the hero model dear to many Americans. Likewise, the similarities between Paul's vision of the universality of sin and Dirty Harry's vision of modern society are at first unnerving. But a careful conversation between the two may help to rescue the concept of the universality of sin from becoming a toothless doctrine, and perhaps it might even render an audience a little less disposed to wreak Dirty Harry's kind of mayhem in Christ's name. If we fail to envision theology in new and, at times, alien narrative images, we will be turning our backs on the scandal of the text and forfeiting the opportunity to say something new; we will be turning the two-edged sword into a butter knife.